PENNY ARCADE™ 3

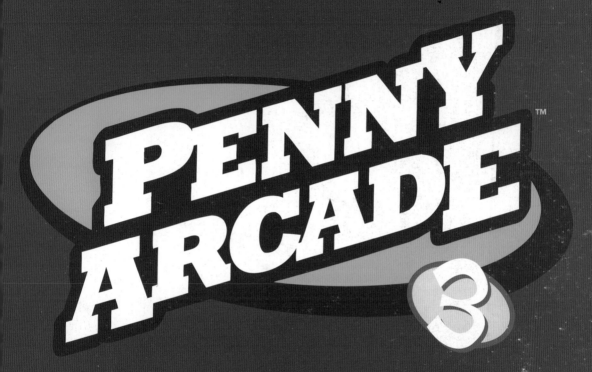

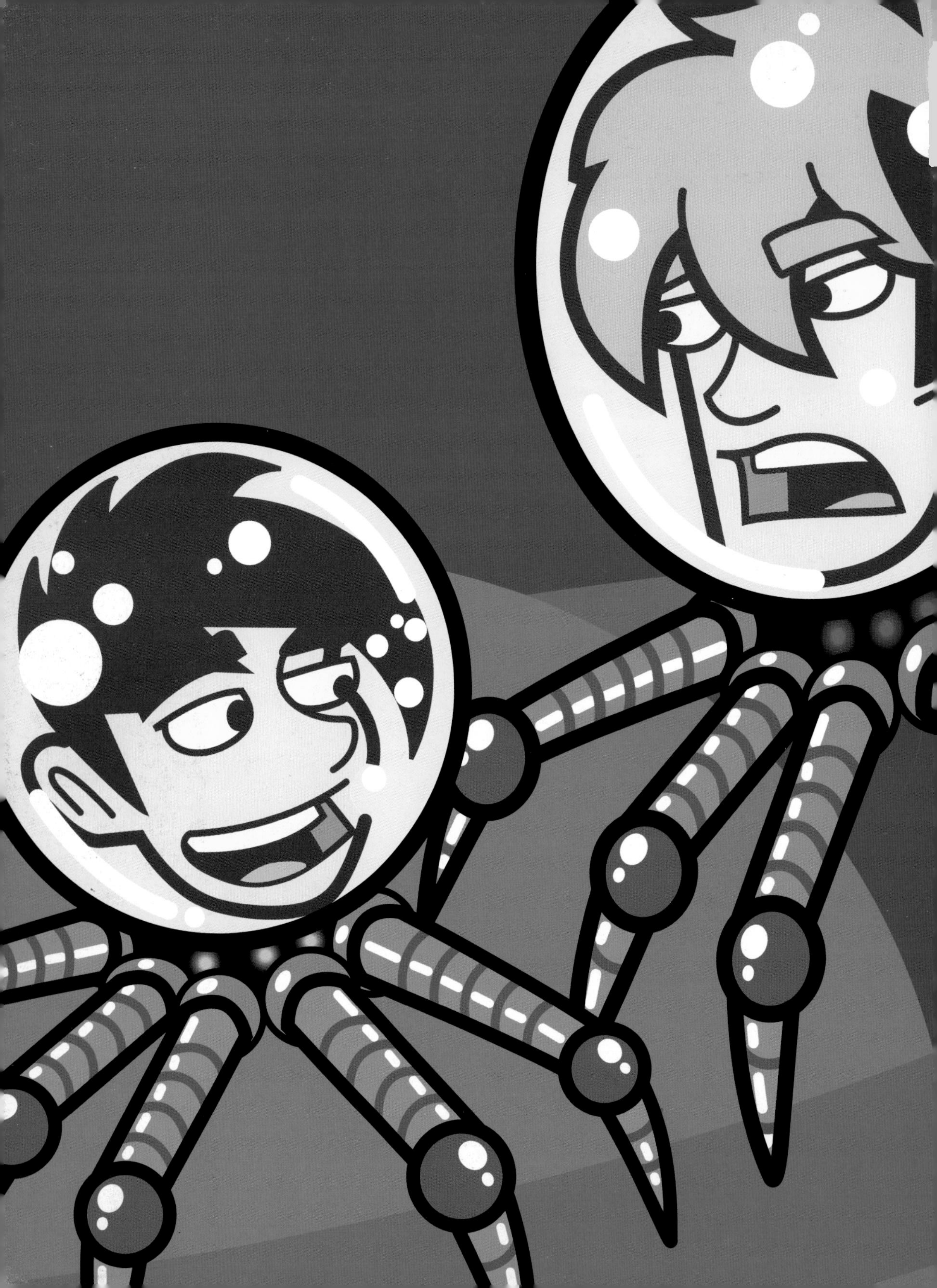

PENNY ARCADE™

PENNY-ARCADE.COM

BY JERRY HOLKINS & MIKE KRAHULIK

dark horse books™

Publisher
MIKE RICHARDSON

Editor
MIKE CARRIGLITTO

Editorial Assistant
SAMANTHA ROBERTSON

Designer
DAVID NESTELLE

Art Director
LIA RIBACCHI

Very special thanks to ROBERT KHOO at *Penny Arcade*!

PENNY ARCADE Volume 3: THE WARSUN PROPHECIES

This volume collects comic strips from the *Penny Arcade* website, originally published online from January 1, 2002 through December 31, 2002.

Published by
Dark Horse Books
A division of Dark Horse Comics, Inc.
10956 SE Main Street
Milwaukie, OR 97222

darkhorse.com

To find a comics shop in your area, call the Comic Shop Locator Service toll-free at 1-888-266-4226

First edition: January 2007
ISBN 10: 1-59307-635-5
ISBN 13: 978-1-59307-635-1

10 9 8 7 6 5 4 3 2 1
Printed in China

Foreword by Scott Kurtz

I have been asked to write the foreword for the third *Penny Arcade* book. What a fucking honor.

I wasn't asked to write the foreword to the first or second book. That went to Bill Amend and J. Allard respectively. Who the fuck is J. Allard? Does anybody know? I guess even the forewords to these books require an accompanying newspost and links to external articles to understand what the fuck is going on.

Regardless, it's good to know that I'm third choice.

You have to understand something . . . I knew these guys before they were rock stars. All you see is the shiny exterior put forth by their crack marketing and PR teams. I know who these bastards really are. They are timid, insecure men who don't even play video games. I'm not kidding. They have a room full of teenagers up in their Seattle compound playing games and writing down their opinions. Jerry just replaces all the small words with big words and posts it to the website. Hand to God. I've seen it.

C'mon guys. Are you really buying into this bullshit persona these two are feeding you? Gabe and Tycho? These guys are not the bad-ass-sons-a-bitches they try to market themselves as. They run a charity for fuck's sake. They are not too cool for school. They liked school. Jerry graduated at the top of his class. It's a well known fact that when these two are not on camera they are actually very kind to children and animals. They're good people. Neither of them have ever set anything on fire. One time Mike tried to blow up some of his army men with firecrackers but backed out at the last minute. He just felt that it was wrong to disrespect those who had truly been blown up in combat.

Let me tell you guys a story of when *PvP* was the crown jewel of webcomics and *Penny Arcade* was just this upstart wanna-be website looking to make a name for itself. What a glorious three months back in 1998 that was. I cherish that feeling and wrap it around myself like a warm blanket.

These days things are little different. *Penny Arcade* is the cool bulldog with the black vest and bowler hat, and I am the small dog yapping at their feet. "We're pals, right, Spike? Right, Spike?" Sure, every once in a while they'll throw me a bone. I think I've been invited to PAX once. Although when I showed up at the door a rather large African-American man insisted my name wasn't on the list. My shoulder still hurts every time it's about to rain.

Some of you may dismiss my words here as the bitter ramblings of an old man who realizes that he's past his prime and will never garner a fraction of the popularity that my peers here at Penny Arcade Incorporated have.

Well, you're correct . . . but try looking at things from my perspective. These are the same guys who, almost eight years ago, signed away their entire creation to a dot-com startup because they thought it was going to make them millionaires. These are the guys who are currently kicking my ass all over the Internet. How would you feel?

I only have one consolation: No matter how many milestones Mike and Jerry beat me to, no matter how popular they become, no matter how much it stings to be left behind in the dust by these two guys . . . I will always be better than *Ctrl-Alt-Del*.

I'm gonna chase that feeling.

Fuck you all for buying this book and not buying *PvP*.

—*Eisner Award Winning Cartoonist*
Scott Richard Kurtz
August 19, 2006
Little Elm, TX

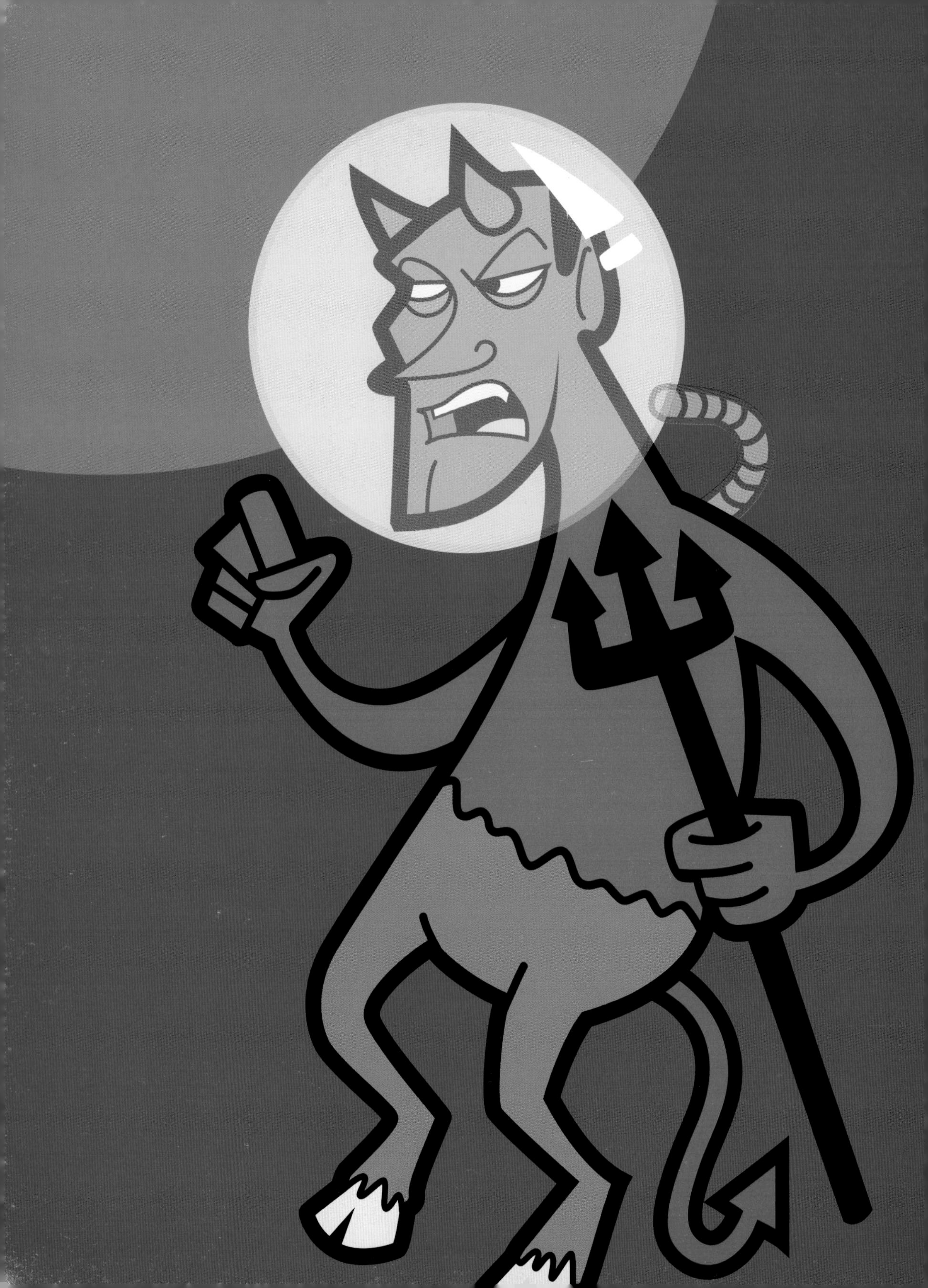

Presenting the Introduction

Wherein the Author Relates a Personal Anecdote of Startling and Perhaps Even Disarming Authenticity

his might be my favorite year of *Penny Arcade*.

I mean, I always like *Penny Arcade*. This having been established, this book represents an odd time in the nine-year history of the project. Being completely reader supported was frightening, in its way—like leaving your destiny up to regional weather patterns. I guess that's what farmers do. I think farming would really freak me out.

But there we were, uploading the JPEGs for which we have become notorious, and somehow it was working. Sometimes people would donate if we'd done a comic they particularly liked. Sometimes they would wait until the end of the month, tally up the ones they had enjoyed, and ascribe a value to them. For many people, that value was exactly *zero*, but who cares? There was something intuitive and correct about the system. It felt right.

We'd begun putting out special art for those who donated, and this also felt right. But the part of the brain that craves security cried out for some kind of *minimum amount* we could bring to the wives, our faces the very image of contrition, evidence that they had not made a terrible decision when they married us.

Eventually we started accepting advertisers, two a month, but "advertisers" is kind of a grand way of putting it. These were just readers who happened to work at game companies. Readers were everywhere! Sometimes, I would open up a drawer and there would be a reader inside.

We had a number of ideas about what to do next, but when simply surviving a given month is your goal it exerts a downward pressure on ambition. That changed when *another* reader asked us to go out to lunch, ostensibly to talk about working together. He could tell within the space of five minutes that we were *idiots*, idiots desperately in need of *help*, like lost pets unaccustomed to the savageries of the actual Earth.

He was not wrong; he was not wrong.

We were *trying* to take it seriously, but as is probably obvious to you, taking things seriously isn't really what we do. After selling the comic strip itself to one fucking guy and selling the book rights to someone (if you can imagine this!) even less capable than we were, it was clear that *we* were actually the worst thing that could happen to *Penny Arcade*. Robert, the man we had met, eventually agreed to be the person who would take things seriously. This seriousness— though not on our part, certainly—brought with it a measure of stability. And from that stability came PAX, the book you are reading, and even Child's Play.

It was a reader who made it happen—and got to us before we managed to destroy the whole thing. One of *you*.

Every good thing that has ever happened to me has been the result of your enthusiasm, your kindness, and your support.

—Tycho Brahe
October 5, 2006
Seattle, WA

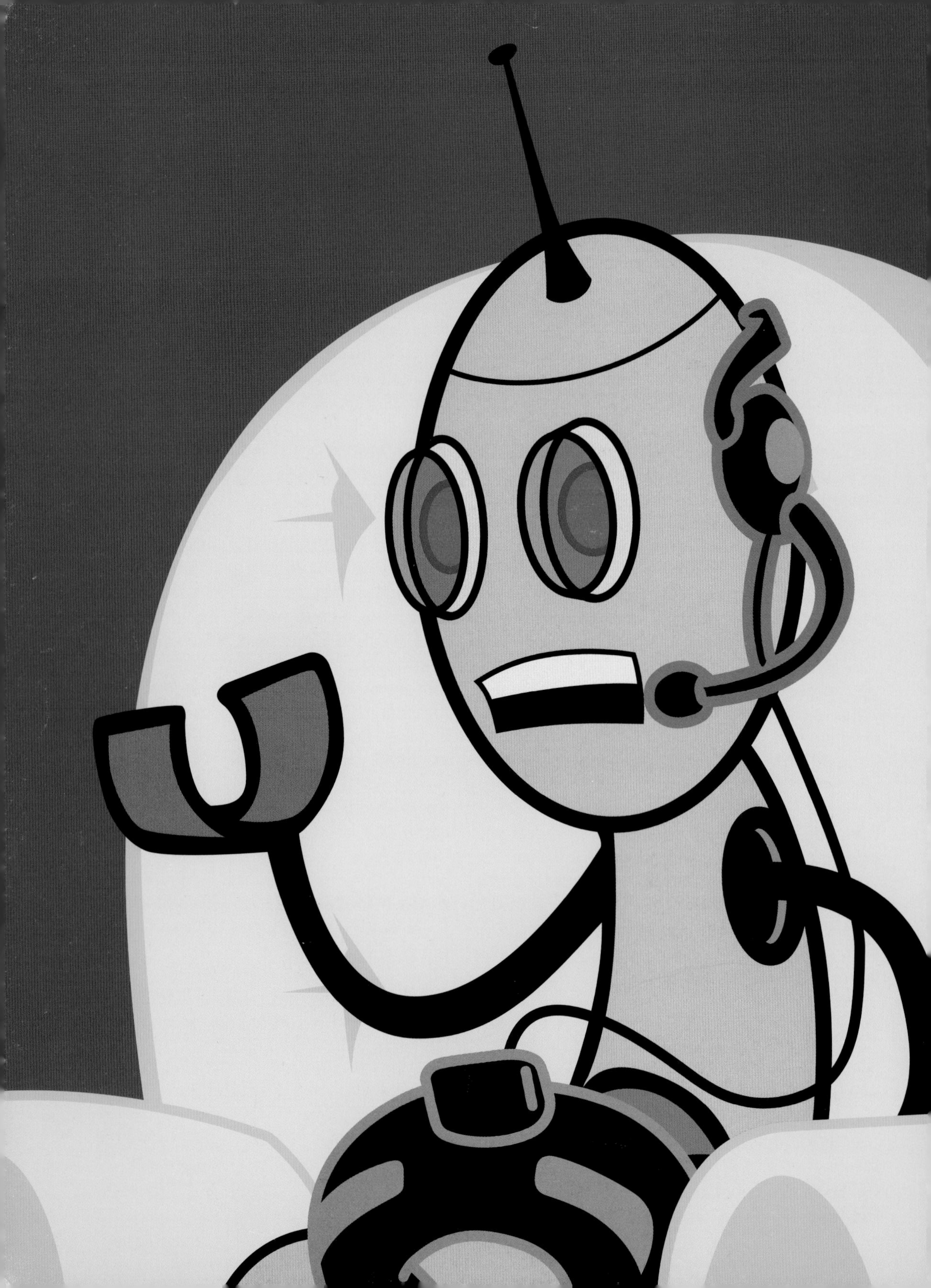

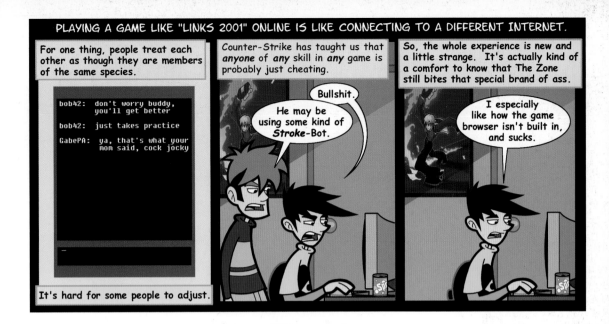

I AM JACK'S GOLF STRIP

January 2, 2002 The people who play online golf in a simmy PC franchise like Links are a completely different group of people than the ones we're usually on a server with. They don't wear *clan tags*. They don't even know what clan tags *are*. They probably think your /\sF/\ SkullFuckers tag is just a typo, the sort of thing that happens when a cat leaps from a monitor onto a keyboard. They don't understand that those slash marks are supposed to be little bat wings.

This experience was just as unnerving as we have implied: I actually *like* how hostile and insular our people can be, and to imagine that this gentle tribe scurries upon the same Web seems impossible. When a stranger is kind to me, I assume they have a friend somewhere with a knife.

These guys were giving club advice, for fuck's sake. They were talking about wind speed and asking if we had any kids. One of them did use a four-letter word—but the word was *bran*. Were we getting enough? These cats were clearly on some Stepford shit. We had to get the F out of there.

IT'S BEEN AWHILE

January 4, 2002 The article we mention in the strip was an interminable sob story about how we were supposed to respect Ion Storm for making bad games. That's the short version, obviously. The final, uncut version of the piece was nearly seven hundred tear-soaked pages, so I have had to condense things somewhat. Also: check out *Masters of Doom*, if you haven't yet. It'll give you some interesting insights into John Romero himself, before the John Romero *persona* rose to dominate the entity.

PENNY ARCADE IS A COMEDY BISTRO

January 6, 2002 I've recently admitted (with no small amount of shame) that I'm just not competition material in most fighters. But there is a period of time, early on, where my erratic attempts at martial combat can trump his tightly focused approach. I savor it, sometimes for an hour or more, and then it is gone.

It didn't used to be like this, but then, fighters didn't used to be like this. I don't know that I've ever really put together a comprehensive philosophy for fighting in three dimensions. The last time I truly felt comfortable in a newer fighter was with the Guilty Gear series, situated (as it is) safely in two dimensions. I was pretty handy at the first few Tekken titles as well, as their gameplay—though rendered in the third *D*—relied upon the traditional forms.

DUCK

January 7, 2002 No doubt it was these formative meetings that would, ultimately, lay the groundwork for John Gabriel's *Greater Internet Fuckwad Theory*. The unique chart really gives the proceedings a sense of gravity, and no doubt the intellectual caliber of the attendees—which is to say, a duck toy and a bear-shaped *rag*—serves to refine the premise.

CHARLITO'S WAY

January 9, 2002 As I sit here typing this very book on one of the new iMacs, I try to cast my mind back to when my resolve first began to weaken. Were the anger and resentment we directed at the platform *actually* the first buds of romance? Was this some weird *thing*, like tugging on a girl's ponytail explicitly *because* you liked her?

THE TIME OF MY LIFE

January 11, 2002 Rez was a fixture for the man. You've probably gotten a good sketch of Gabe over the years, enough to know that this kind of devotion to a single player game just doesn't happen. Most "rhythm games," Bemani, what have you, use rhythm as a means to judge the quality of player input. By contrast, Rez is a game *about* rhythm, in which the player *inhabits* music. I'll take the second one.

ANOTHER TRUE STORY

January 14, 2002 The blinding illumination of this experience has dulled somewhat over the last four years. You may be better served by an ancient version of myself, those shocking tastes still upon his lips:

I'm getting my chicken soup on, it's Sunday afternoon, and Gabe's reading some *Preacher* in the den, which is also the living room, the bathroom, and the foyer. I am interacting with pasta dough in what I think is a stern way, when I hear him say that he might like the soup better if it were, in fact, carrot cake. It hits us, hits us both simultaneously, like a semi made out of lightning, which is also a professional boxer. Carrot Cake Soup. You cube the carrot cake, some pieces have frosting and some don't, and you put a handful of these chunks into a bowl full of milk. So let's go do it. We'll do it later this week, he says. But I know that's the same as not doing it. Why not now, I say? I know a store where we can get all the stuff. You can just buy it, the way you can buy stuff in the household cleaners section and make a bomb big enough to kill God. The stuff is just lying around there and nobody's doing anything with it. It's not a crime to buy them separately, and what we do at home isn't any of their fucking business.

I think someone might have been following us as we pulled into the parking lot. We walked toward the grocery store and tried to keep the conversation natural. We certainly didn't discuss *carrot*

cake or the *soup* one might make by cutting it into cubes and swimming islands of it in cold milk, pleasure islands, like you'd see in a magazine. At the bakery counter, a woman asks if she can help me, and I'm so nervous that as I'm pointing to the carrot cake behind the glass, my finger starts to tap in Morse code that reads:

I AM ABOUT TO COMMIT A CRIME AGAINST GOD AND MAN STOP

And where is Gabe with that Goddamn milk? There he is, in the self-checkout. *Idiot.* There are cameras all over that thing; it's like a Goddamn surveillance tree. It doesn't take a genius to put two and two together. A red light flashes on, and *off* in my mind. At another checkstand, I pay with untraceable cash, assuring the woman that I will eat the cake by myself, without assistance from cows. I smirk. This woman has no idea that she's just sold me the trigger to a flavor gun.

Carrot Cake Soup is like the taste of watching girls make out. It has an extraordinary power that oscillates between gentle and overwhelming, between light and dark, between pleasure and more pleasure. When it was over, I realized that I was panting. I was in possession of carnal knowledge. And I knew that, somehow, every taste beyond this point was in the service of the one that still lingered, waited, to remind me that nature has laws, and those that break them are criminals, and though they roam free enough the *knowing* will hold them, and keep them, until the last.

IT'S A PROBLEM

January 16, 2002 Strangely enough, he's the only person I *don't* refer to by his handle. A console gamer at heart, in the age before consoles were on good terms with the Internet, I actually had to teach him *about* handles and their critical importance. If we'd met in a digital context (as so often happens these days) I imagine that our handles would simply be the default, and our Christian names would have dried up and fallen off.

THE FURTHER ADVENTURES OF

January 18, 2002 We eventually did pick up SimGolf, and it did dominate us, just as was foretold by the ancient scrolls. I mean it. It was a complete mess. We uploaded an early version of our course to the site, the legendary "Heritage Hills," and our mania was apparent. There was a tangle of shrubs on the third hole that, when the camera was zoomed all the way out, read "Oh God, Please Help."

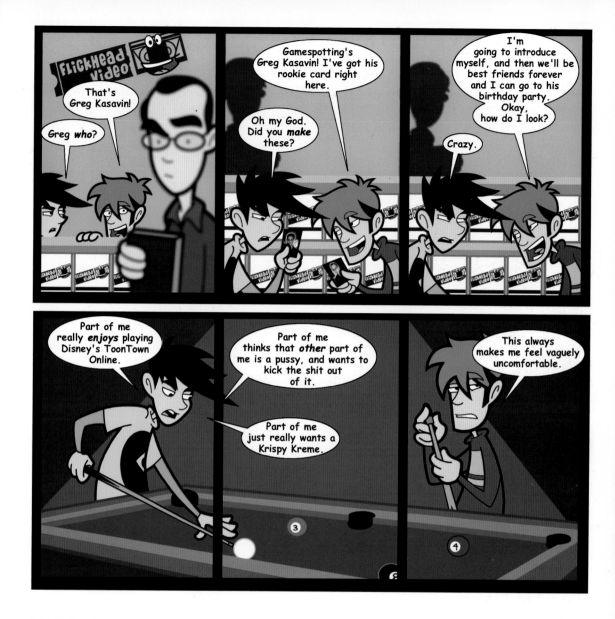

LIKE FIRE

January 21, 2002 It's not a joke. There was a time in my life when, as is natural for a young man, I became obsessed with the editor of a gaming website. "Kasavin" is a beefy, Eastern European sounding name with so much *meat* on it that I could just say it over and *over* and it would be like eating at a buffet.

THERE'S NO Q IN CUE

January 23, 2002 People are still playing it, actually—Disney's Toontown, I mean. It's addictive in all the ways MMOs tend to be. When we first tried the open beta, it was full of emissaries from the Internet's dedicated gamer contingent. Seeing an adorable blue dog wearing its Super X-Hardcore clan tag still brings a smile to my face.

THERE WILL BE A TEST

January 25, 2002 This is an important thing to keep in mind: that *already*, even by the Year of our Lord Two Thousand and Two, people were getting sick of World War II games. It is (at the time of this writing) four years hence, and there has been NO INTERRUPTION in the DELUGE!

THEY'RE REALLY LONG

January 28, 2002 I'm not really in a position to make fun of people who play Magic, or indeed, any collectible card game. Or people who wear all black. Or people who live at their parents' house longer than is strictly necessary. And, you know what? Honestly? Been kinda thinkin' about a wallet chain.

PROJEKT BULLSHIT

January 30, 2002 There was a concert tour at the time associated with Nintendo called Projekt: Revolution. It featured Linkin Park, and what we learned from this comic is that people get really mad if you make fun of things that are tangentially related to a band that they like. Linkin Park inspires this kind of loyalty with their anthemic sound and incisive lyrics, like those on "Whore": "Won't clean my room / Never clean my room / Won't clean it never ever / Mom you are dumb."

JUST A RUMOR THOUGH

February 1, 2002 The name of the strip is actually a lyric from a House of Pain song. There are a number of weird "word games" we play all the time, games we never really defined but have been playing for twelve or more years, and many of those games revolve around bits of lyrics. The categories tend to fall into rhyming games, memorization games, and syncopation games. It's kind of strange now that I think of it, but I guess they're a kind of writing calisthenics.

BOBA FETT IS © 2002 LUCASFILM LTD

February 4, 2002 "Sending ideas to LucasArts" was something we had goofed around with as a comic concept for a while, but sending complete game designs with full concept art is something he has actually done. When one of his more recent treatises on the Star Wars Expanded Universe material was replied to with an *extremely* legal cease and desist type mail, we put this one together. I guess they didn't like it? It was a Wookiee Jedi sports team management simulator.

THE NEXT LEVEL

February 6, 2002 SOE decided that one way to make a lot more money would be to charge people forty dollars a month to play Everquest. They set up special servers where they would pamper your characters with exotic, presumably imported bits, not the common bits of questionable purity players on other servers had to contend with. When they allowed character transfers, those servers became ghost towns. I guess technically they would be *luxury* ghost towns.

HMM, INDEED

February 8, 2002 Maximo was hard—a coarser man might even call it *bitch* hard. I am not that man! For one thing, I am not coarse. From head to toe, I am as smooth as marble.

For another thing, I didn't actually play it so much as I watched my ally Gabriel be mutilated by it. One does not see a trusted friend eviscerated, and then present one's own belly, as if to say "Please let me have some of *that.*"

Drawing great handfuls of Beef Jerky from a Ziploc bag, I believe I weakly offered, "Damn, man . . . Skeletons, you know? Yow . . ." or something to that effect. I'm not sure he was particularly bolstered by it. Then again, he looked to be tying a noose there with the cable of his DualShock, so I think he was at a *low point.*

WOW

February 11, 2002 Yes, well . . . Hmm. Die Hard was not a very good game, and the relatively primitive version of LithTech that powered it did not set the heart ablaze. But I must say, I almost forgot there was even a reference to it in here. This many years later, only the Fruit Fucker itself remains.

V-DAY

February 13, 2002 We thought we'd celebrate Valentine's Day the traditional way, with heartfelt sentiments directed toward the developers and designers that had filled us with such longing. Gabe's is clearly the more accomplished of the two, but I think my powerful imagery really takes it home. Of course, the real meat of 2015 would leave after this and form Infinity Ward, of (considerable) Call of Duty fame. I had to fill out a small form, but I was able to transfer the love.

A CAUTIONARY NOTE

February 15, 2002 Triton Labs' legendary *Afterburner* product was a somewhat odd creature, made almost necessary by the extremely poor visibility of the original Game Boy Advance. That ill-favored machine was replaced not once but *twice*, with two separate versions of the SP, and fully three times if we consider the Nintendo DS to be its true successor. We'll go into specifics in a short while, but the installation of this contraption proved to be something of a black art.

NOUVEAU NOVIO

February 18, 2002 Critical to the crew *system* we had in place was the voice server, and not logging into it created situations like this one. These days it's TeamSpeak or one of the modern equivalents, but none of these products have the simplicity or the humanity of the old Sidewinder GameVoice. I like how it worked, to be sure, but I think also that you just get used to the way an audio codec *presents* your friends.

NUMQUESTIONS = 20

February 20, 2002 We weren't reading comics in his room; we were driving from Spokane to Seattle. Once you make that minor transposition, the round went precisely as you see it presented here. Familiarity, beyond a certain point, becomes indistinguishable from *psychic mind beams*.

OFF-OFF-OFF-OFF-BROADWAY

February 22, 2002 Awful! Good Lord, was it fucking awful. One would imagine that ultraviolence and shrieking crowds would be the electronic equivalent of chocolate and peanut butter! Nay, sir—and again, I say *nay*. There was even a sequel produced. It went through three publishers, two developers, and bankruptcy only to be released—ultimately—by its true master, he who is called Satan the Devil.

JUST LIKE YOU REMEMBER, # 2

February 25, 2002 There was a watch reference a couple strips ago, and just seeing that time-piece gets us in the mood for slaughter. Also, if stuffing a person into a dumpster seems like a good time to you, you might grab one of the Hitman games. That's basically what they're about.

OBSCURE REFERENCES WEEK CONT.

February 27, 2002 I love the idea that *Penny Arcade's* Kool-Aid thin continuity is so rich, with so many critical junctures, that you must have a tiny sidebar (like the one in the last panel) to have any hope of navigating its forked path. Some firebrands raise this aggressive, almost enforced transience as evidence of our . . . something. I didn't really understand what they were talking about. No doubt their ten readers agreed *wholeheartedly*.

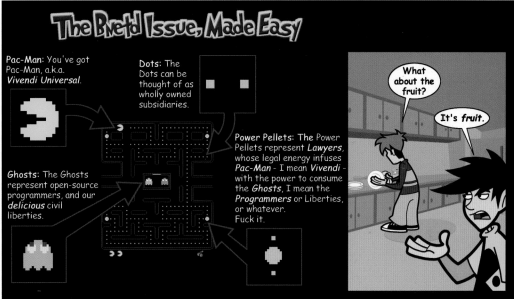

PLEASE, CALL ME KOTOR

March 1, 2002 I think history has spoken with clarity on the subject of Gabriel's "strength" in this matter. Star Wars *was* a cruel trick though, all told. You already know about his Endor bed sheets and the Wookiee straw, so we need not tarry long on that topic. But his *protocol droid*—the one he brings to work? It's not a protocol droid. It's a store mannequin lacquered in Dutch Boy Gold.

IT STARTS WITH B

March 4, 2002 Bnetd was a program that emulated Blizzard's Battle.net, allowing players to set up their own unauthorized versions of the service. The strip itself, with its rabble-rousing language, is clearly in support of the project—but not being a lawyer myself, I mused on the actual legalities in play within the post. This was a mistake. Thousands of angry e-mails later, I would learn that the right to hack a gaming network is considered a fundamental civil liberty.

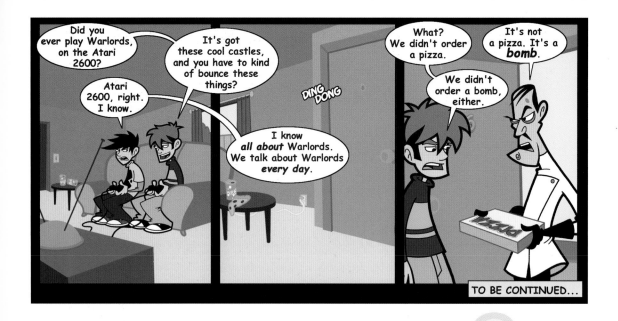

DAS OLDSKOOLEN, PART ONE

March 6, 2002 It may interest you to know what odd alchemies are required to produce strips like this one and the one that follows it.

My obsession with Warlords on the Atari 2600 is not some kind of joke. It's a genuine condition that I have been treated for. I take each day one at a time, now. I try not to think about the paddle in my grip, the wheel of it spinning free. I should be able to tell you the basics without a dangerous lapse: Warlords is essentially a four-player game of the classic Breakout, where each player assumes a quadrant of the screen and tries to defend their castle. I'm always bringing it up, but since it was released in the dark period before the inception of *Penny Arcade*, there was no opportunity to mention it. I had to invent one, and there you have it.

As for Mordo himself, "Mordo" was our nemesis in online rounds of Medal of Honor: Allied Assault. He just happened to play on *every server* we joined, and to confront him in a ruined French alleyway was to face death itself. At the same time, we'd created a kind of soul-reaping demon (we do that sometimes) named Baelzebob who always felt a little bad about his job and did his best to be polite and accommodating about it. As we were sitting down to write the strip that day all of this stuff became conflated somehow, as it is wont to do. Man, shit is *always* getting conflated around here.

DAS OLDSKOOLEN, PART TWO

March 8, 2002

SITTING IN A TREE

March 11, 2002 Nintendo fans really needed an infusion in those days, and so if they wore elaborate hats from time to time I can find it in my heart to forgive them. The arrangement largely amounted to ports of archival games to Nintendo's Game Boy Advance systems, but Final Fantasy: Crystal Chronicles—a game you either really "got" or absolutely hated—spun in our GameCube, proud and unchallenged, for weeks on end.

THE LIGHTSABER SAYS

March 13, 2002 After having been brutalized by every employer on Earth, the moon, and indeed some of the far-flung Deepstar colonies, we decided that Gabriel should see at least some affection in this life: this is the power of *fiction*.

RE RE

March 15, 2002 They keep making them, so someone must be watching them, If only for Milliana Jovolovovich. Speaking about *The Wizard* in particular, showings of that film are now a cultural event every year at PAX. It would not surprise me if, after a couple more years, *Wizard* Watching became a true ritual of its own: people acting out parts, lines shouted at the screen, etc. I can't wait.

PSO REVISITED

March 18, 2002 Long after it had passed into memory for most people, we hauled out our Dreamcasts, wiped the dust from our PSO platters, and coaxed the readership online with their now ancient equipment. We urged a return to those simpler times, when all you needed were a couple hungry Mags and a pack full of Moon Atomizers to feed them.

THE Y IS SILENT

March 20, 2002 Bloodrayne was a controversial title —there are simply strong opinions in play when you're dealing with kung-fu Nazi vampire hookers. I have no serious complaint about the series. Indeed, I might even have a few compliments. But letting the savage and bestial Uwe Boll obtain the license, and then make some kind of medieval porn movie? Be not proud.

CHOOSE YOUR CHARACTER

March 22, 2002 You can see the Stone of the Ages that collects our greatest fighting game rivalries there in panel two—from top to bottom, it goes Samurai Shodown, Street Fighter Alpha, Tekken (Import), Zero Divide, Killer Instinct, and Soul Calibur II. I eventually got to keep Lei Fei, by the way. I just kept choosing him over and over again, driving Gabriel into a rage, to which I would respond with an expression that said, "Have I offended you? I can't imagine how."

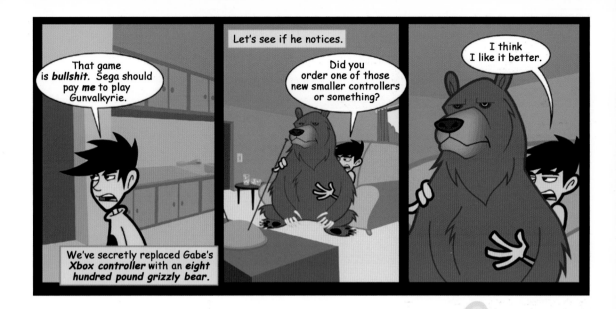

URSINE ADVENTURES

March 25, 2002 This comic was originally designed to bring the "large controller comics" era to an end. It was a very productive period, and certainly while securing a bear was *extremely* expensive we wanted to really cap the whole shebang with something spectacular. Except that only a month later, we would fall back on our old tricks—diminishing our substantial investment.

We've made the most of him, though—Barnum. By which I mean *the bear*.

Oh, yes—we still have him! Having a bear with you opens doors, it just does. And those doors that *remain* closed are smashed into splinters by a snarling, hairy wall of meat. When you ride a bear to the mall, you don't park him. You just ride him straight in through the automatic doors. I've grown almost addicted to the respect and consideration I get when cruising around on a bear. I usually wear a cape as well; I think it completes the look, but I know deep down that the cape isn't the main factor.

FANTASTIC STORIES, # 1

March 27, 2002 It may come as a surprise to you, but I was fixated on Irrational Games' super-hero strategy romp, Freedom Force. And the sequel, Freedom Force vs. The Third Reich. Also, I'm tentatively obsessed with whatever game they might release in the future.

DON'T LISTEN TO HIM

March 29, 2002 For whatever reason, most likely the work of authors devoted to Star Wars as a storytelling context, he has retained his enthusiasm—but the man has limits. I would guess that watching Lando Calrissian swing a saber around would be the same as seeing him do a lip trick off a Rancor and then grind on a flying skiff for maximum points. I hope he doesn't read that last sentence, as it would probably kill him.

ALL TEETH ACCOUNTED FOR

April 1, 2002 He's moved three times since this comic, and I swear to God *the magazines are still coming.*

TWH: VOLUME ONE

April 3, 2002 The incendiary reaction to the first volume of the series makes me glad that, even four years out, we never delivered the second installment.

I was under the impression that we were making a statement about a genre of art, i.e. "We think that pictures of eroticized, bipedal animals are ridiculous." What we would come to find out was that this kind of imagery is a cultural signifier for a group of people—"furries"—for whom this material amounts to some kind of sacrament.

So, imagine my surprise when we received hundreds of mails suggesting that we were "bigots," which is not a word *I* associate with people who think pictures of impossible animals are silly. The discourse was fascinating. I'm not difficult to talk to, and once it became clear that I had discovered something completely unlike anything I knew, I began to interrogate the authors of the hate mail themselves. I made about a hundred friends in a couple hours, people I talked to for years.

What I think is funny about the strip is that it purports to make some kind of strong point in the first panel, and then invests the remainder of its short time with the reader running away from this point at top speed. Of course, if you only look at the first panel and then send an angry mail, it doesn't matter. There are very few things we can actually say we hate, and a picture of two gazelles on a first date hardly makes the cut.

THE SIGN DOES NOT LIE

April 5, 2002 Dungeon Siege came with an entire extra world you could play with friends, and the (ahem) "Pit of Despair" was and *is* a dark, dark hole full of nothing. Leaving him to die alone and without precious light probably doesn't make me a very good friend, but I've rarely been accused of *that*.

X PLUS WHORES EQUALS

April 8, 2002 We've made more than one comic about the bitching that is so commonplace on every server, for every game, every day and all night. If you are doing too well, this is a reason for someone to complain. If you aren't doing well enough, someone else will take their turn. If you've selected a weapon they don't like—a weapon that is available to them as well, but one that they don't approve of because of some imaginary online *martial code*—then here comes more bullshit. I haven't looked at playertext for years, and I've been healthier for it.

THE GAME DETECTIVE, PART ONE

April 10, 2002 Once there was a gamer network, clearly this meant gamer *shows*, and we had an idea hot to go. *The Game Detective*. We only got three strips out of it, but I think the major points came across. We eventually got into a huge fight with somebody from G4, but we get into huge fights with everybody so it hardly bears mentioning.

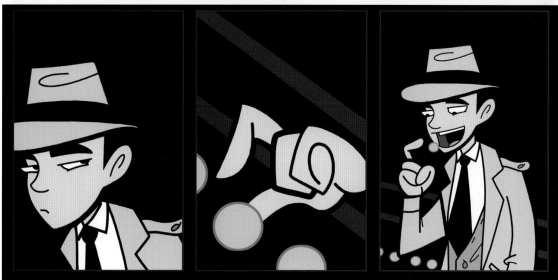

THE GAME DETECTIVE, PART TWO

April 12, 2002 One of the major points I was trying to get across was that Gabe is a know-nothing asshole. It's a theme I've tried to *weave* throughout my writing.

THE GAME DETECTIVE, PART THREE

April 15, 2002 This is one of my top five strips for some reason. Who hasn't wondered what those things taste like? Are they kosher? I have a hard time picturing every single dot being authenticated by a rabbinical process.

RESIDENT, UH . . . SOMETHING

April 17, 2002 Ultimately, the term *bullshot* would be coined to describe materials that had been falsified in some way—specifically, falsified upwards in terms of quality. But this screen they released for REO was almost completely unintelligible, and may necessitate the creation of a new word to describe the opposite effect.

DEAR LORD

April 19, 2002 Soldier of Fortune II—a game that wasn't even supposed to have multiplayer—delivered online action that demanded to be taken seriously. The brutality referred to above was part of the experience, certainly—but the tight level design and visceral, high-impact weapons dominated our LAN parties for years.

PAY ATTENTION

April 22, 2002 Frustrated by accusations of "camping"—a contentious online slur—we prepared this devastating response. The term camping literally has no meaning in this context, where one team must explicitly defend and the other must explicitly attack. Know that these were base and rowdy men who, having accrued many losses by our sure hand, tried to shift the battle with rhetoric rather than skill. They met with no success.

IT'S TOO DAMN LATE

April 24, 2002 I can break this down for you, easy. Panel One: The Xbox is big. Panel Two: God damn is it big! It is big for *reals*. Panel Three: There was a pretty fresh mod making the rounds at the time that combined a PC, an Atari 2600, an Xbox, a GameCube, an NES, and a PS2 all in the same physical box. And the bass guitar? The bass guitar is there to *shame Gabe*.

SEEMS WET

April 26, 2002 After Judge Stephen Limbaugh declared that video games were not subject to free speech protections because they were "not capable of communicating ideas," we decided that the only proper response would be one of those terrible editorial cartoons you see in the paper.

We were able to get our hands on the actual decision in this case from a "lawyer friend." It included a list of games the judge had examined to arrive at this conclusion: Mortal Combat, Fear Effect, DOOM, and The Resident of Evil Creek.

As I said at the time, one of those isn't even a game. Imagine if a person with an axe to grind against cinema—ridiculous, right?—made legally binding declarations about all movies based on only *Armageddon, Dumb and Dumberer, DOOM*, and *Batman & Robin*?

This Culture War bullshit is starting to drive me nuts. I'd go live in a *cave* somewhere if I thought I could find one with DSL.

SOMETIMES THINGS COST MONEY

April 29, 2002 This comic did not ingratiate us with a certain segment of the readership, it's true, but as two people living off the service we provided online, the idea that someone might need to charge for something wasn't an act we could really fault them for.

I WILL CHOKE HIM

May 1, 2002 Playing Resident Evil games as a (for lack of a better term) "couple" has been a tradition going back, well, back to the first Alone in the Dark game, where the Resident Evil franchise actually started. You can see here that he made poor choices. It was worth the wait, though: if you're going to remake an old game practically room for room, Resident Evil on the Cube is *precisely* how you do it.

RESIDENT EVIL, ADDENDUM

May 3, 2002 This is what I am *trying* to do every time I open up notepad and start to write something for the site. And when I succeed, it feels like someone else wrote it, and I can't take credit for it. This is what it's like to be a crazy person: I can go back through the archive, like I am now, and actually feel intimidated by my own Goddamn work.

WHAT, INDEED, PART ONE

May 6, 2002 There are a bunch of things that we imply about the world these *versions* of ourselves live in, and they're things that I don't always rationally agree with, but they're true in the context. For example, Tycho manages to be a staunch atheist even though Jesus (who is the Christ) comes over to his house once a week, at *minimum*. We're implying something else here that isn't really that hard to pick up.

WHAT, INDEED, PART TWO

May 7, 2002 After we had written this comic, Gabriel spent the entire afternoon writing different versions of the last panel that had the term "hard cocks" replaced with various innocuous
things. Every fifteen or twenty minutes he would send one to me with the pleading subject line,
"better?" or somesuch, but I already had the one I wanted. Hard Cocks 4 Life!

ATTACK OF THE CLOWNS

May 10, 2002 Listening to Gabriel's increasingly desperate defense of these movies ceased
being the *delicious meal* it was originally and eventually just bummed me out. This proud thing
was being dismantled right in front of him, and the entire process was subsidized by the faithful.

THE GRIM SCHEMATIC

May 13, 2002 We actually *did* have a complete plan that incorporated all these things. They were not meant to be absolutely random, but any evil diagrams we might have generated are now lost to time. They may be unearthed when Seattle is the site of an archaeological dig, but given my city's proximity to the ocean it may be less of a dig and more of a Special Television Event, like when they sent little subs into the Titanic to get all those spoons.

GOING DOWN

May 15, 2002 I love Frank. I could go on, but it would all be variations on that phrase and honestly I think people would catch on pretty quick.

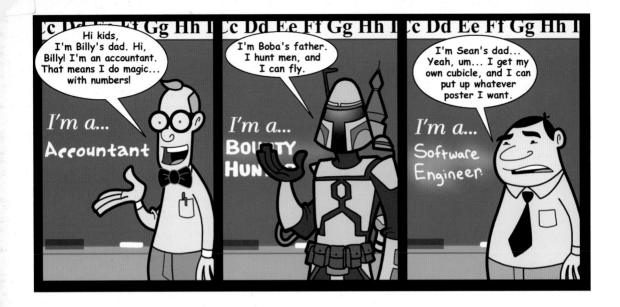

FETTISH

May 17, 2002 I find the last panel of this comic very, very depressing.

We didn't realize it at the time, because Karen Traviss wouldn't write her excellent *Republic Commando* novels until years later, but putting Jango Fett (and, indeed, Mandalorians in general) in a paternal context is something that has a lot of power.

I wouldn't have called it, either. But she managed to take something as "manufactured" as a clone army and really give it life, by inventing a warrior culture and language that prizes fatherhood. Her books *Hard Contact* and *Triple Zero* cover highly idiosyncratic groups of clone troopers—of which *Republic Commando's* Delta Squad is one—raised not as *soldiers* by hardened Mando mercenaries, but as sons.

Before I had a son of my own, this stuff might have seemed like cheap sentimentality. After the first couple times I spoke to him in affectionate Mandalorian I began to perceive that the books had resonated deeply.

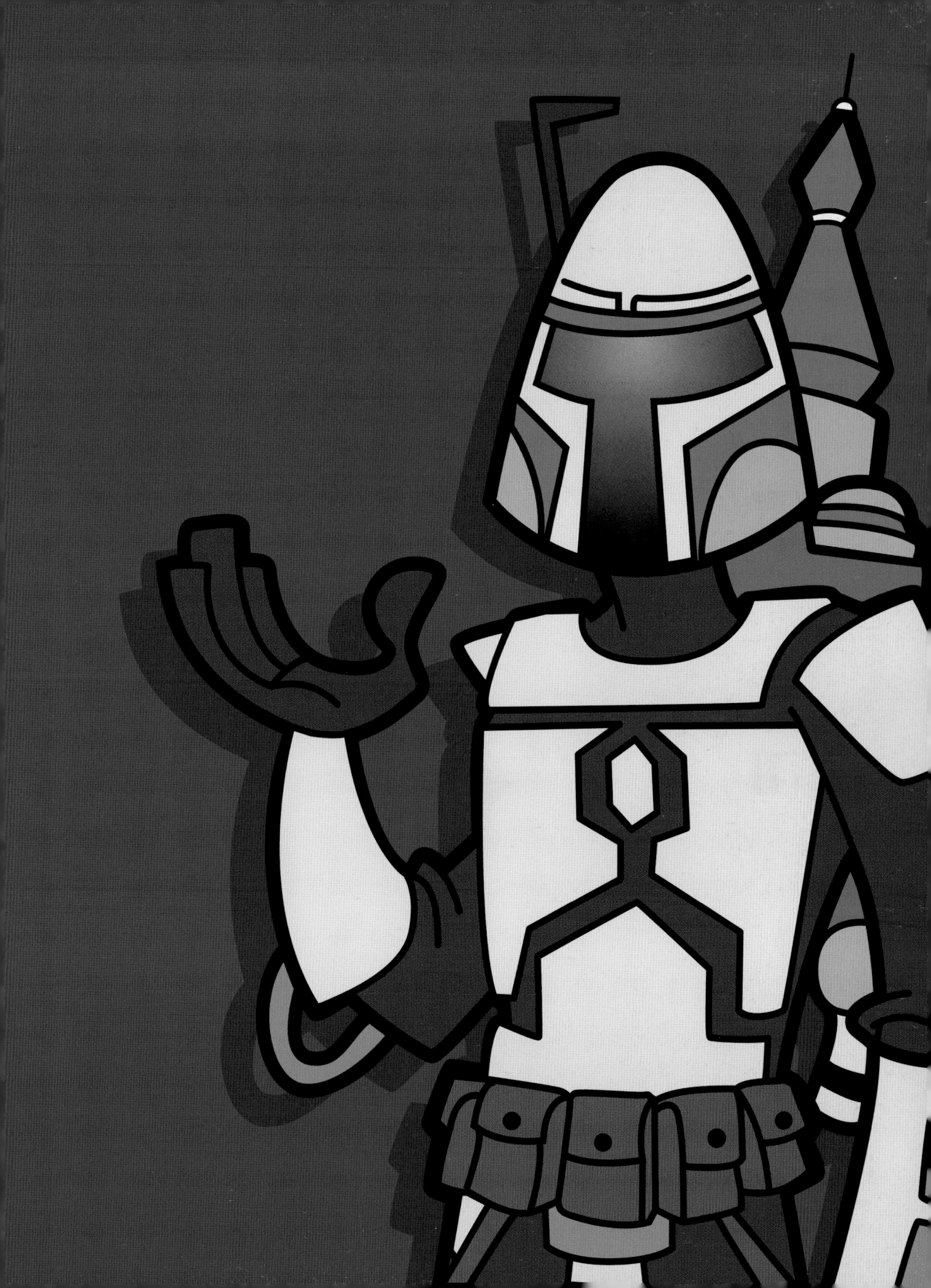

PENNY ARCADE'S
AFTERBURNER
INSTALLATION MANUAL

1 Be sure that you have the necessary tools for the installation, such as a Dremel™, Soldering Iron, Bizarre Security Screwdriver, Flux, Exacto Knife, and Leprechaun.

2 Throw all that shit in the garbage.

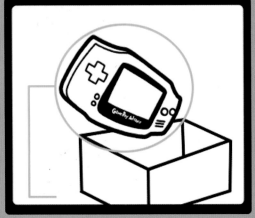

3 Put Your Game Boy Advance™ in a box and send it to someone who knows what the *fuck* they're doing.

4 What the *hell* is wrong with you?

ADDENDUM TO THE MANUAL

May 20, 2002 These events are not terribly ancient, but since you might not have been crazy enough to do it *yourself* at the time, a little extra information might be prudent.

The Afterburner was a mod you could purchase for your GBA. It came in a plastic bag that appeared to contain random bits of junk you might find stuck to some gum beneath the counter at a filthy diner. As we suggested in an earlier volume—and, indeed, a few pages ago in the tome that sits before you—the Game Boy Advance excelled in many things, got good grades, cleaned its plate, etc., but unless conditions were absolutely perfect you could not *see* the events that occurred on-screen. This was a grim outcome for such a promising thingamajig.

After much precision grinding, cutting, and soldering, you either (a) ruined your portable, or (b) created a machine that, while *improved*, was still nowhere as good as the SP. Our friend Pork ended up installing six or seven of these things, perfecting the procedure, and turning out really clean product.

Let me draw your attention to the leprechaun in panels one and two, as it was through a strange and wondrous currency that I was able to secure that tiny man. Behold:

CONCEPT COUPON

PRESENT THIS COUPON TO YOUR ARTIST AND RECEIVE ONE (1) OF YOUR VISUAL CONCEPTS IMPLEMENTED IN A CARTOON STRIP.

CONCEPTS THAT MAY BE IMPLEMENTED INCLUDE BUT ARE NOT LIMITED TO: HAND GESTURES OR FACIAL EXPRESSIONS FOR CHARACTERS, LOCATIONS OR ACTIVITIES, CLOTHING OR ACCESSORIES.

Limit one coupon per person, per day. This coupon has absolutely no cash value. Non-transferable. Void where prohibited. This coupon may not be used in conjunction with other coupons, offers or promotional programs. This coupon is not good if the artist is in an especially poor mood.

Gabe's only given me two of them, ever. So any weird thing you see in *Penny Arcade* these days is his fault—and his alone!

E32K2: UNCLE

May 22, 2002 We wrote this one after seeing America's Army for the first time. Most of the guys we met that day went on to form a new developer called Scion, which eventually got snapped up by Epic and did some really cool stuff for them. We were trying to figure out exactly how the game's strong patriotic message would sync up with the kind of discourse you find in most games.

Gabriel Interviews A Producer On Star Wars: Galaxies

E32K2: WUV

May 23, 2002 This was back when there was still some faith in it. I think we can be forgiven for believing that an MMO based on *Star Wars* seemed like something worth investigating.

E32K2: NOW WITH MORE DOOM

May 24, 2002 And many years later, of course, they did: Prey and Quake Wars both put the tech to quite engaging use.

E32K2: OVER THERE

May 25, 2002 I have no idea how we come across to people who aren't used to us. I would guess badly, but I really *do* want to know what snacks people eat, or if they have Mentadent over there, or if they use gel or mousse. It is with these seemingly disparate data points that I triangulate the soul of a nation.

ADVENTURES

May 27, 2002 In reality, we sat quietly in line waiting to meet Bruce Campbell. We'd seen him the previous year and the line scared us away, and we determined that *this* year, by God, we would manage that beast. While we were in line, we met a couple readers—one of whom kept leaving the line briefly and returning with riches beyond compare. We felt compelled to immortalize it.

SWITCHEROO

May 29, 2002 I'd forgotten that it was Panzer Dragoon Orta that hauled him over to the green-and-black side early. It's an Xbox classic in my opinion—a great rail shooter with an understated story. Man, I should go dig that back out. I hope I've still got my save; there was some really interesting bonus content.

THE CYCLE, PART ONE

May 31, 2002 Before he was able to recognize that RPGs constituted another genre, with its own advantages and disadvantages, one he could select games from if he felt like it, he just had these *random fits* of RPG play—spasms whose origin I could never quite determine. In the strip, I suggest that the flap of a butterfly's wings, a celestial conflux, and a magic clock striking *simultaneously* are somehow responsible. Your guess is as good as mine.

THE CYCLE, PART TWO

June 3, 2002 In this case, the *confluence* was short-lived.

I was glad we had an opportunity to mention Merlyn's, though. I don't know what the "scene" over in Spokane is like these days, but Merlyn's sold comics as well as tabletop games and had, for some reason, a used role-playing books section that was uncommonly full of ancient gems. It was the sort of place you sold your old stuff to when you got out of the hobby, secure in the knowledge that your prized campaigns and supplements would find a good home.

Now that we're paying sixty dollars per game—how dated that reference will appear to our progeny!—it's hard to imagine that, with an investment of only twenty or so dollars, you could buy a book that would keep you and your friends entertained for years.

Clearly there are other costs: additional supplements for example, and of course the social cost incurred by being a basement-dwelling dice addict. I haven't been able to seriously commit to a campaign in a while now, but I still keep up with the books. I don't know why. Part of it is probably some reflex. Part of it is that, you know, once the *bombs* fall, I think I'm going to have a lot of free time.

THE SUM OF ALL STUFF

June 5, 2002 It comes up again sometimes, usually when someone has just learned of it. But America's Army—the *game*—has been called everything from "propaganda" to "other words that also mean propaganda." Practically every videogame on the market lionizes those who serve in the military, be it in the past, present, or future. America's Army actually makes it seem *less* glamorous than most.

HE'S GOT LEGS

June 7, 2002 Their apartment was perpetually crawling with hairy arachnids, their plump abdomens quivering. After having professional insect destruction experts ply their trade on more than one occasion, they eventually just moved out, ceding victory to the creatures. Spiders even send him cards sometimes. I think they miss him, in their way.

QUOTE NEWS UNQUOTE

June 10, 2002 Gabe thinks that Randy Pinkwood is just pure amusement every time, and is always trying to include him, but I make him jump through these little hoops to get him. For example—and this is only an example, unconnected to anything—I might suggest that the network try to (perhaps unsuccessfully) set him up with a partner.

ACTIVATE

June 12, 2002 Not having any prior knowledge of these Wonder Twins, I listened with growing horror as Gabriel described their . . . their *activities*. They had apparently been picked up for a film around this time, but I haven't heard anything since. I think we know why.

NOSTALGIA WEEK CONTINUES

June 14, 2002 Still no M.A.S.K., Goddammit! No M.A.S.K. after these long, dark years. And don't even *start* me on fucking Centurions, man. I've heard it said that what the world needs now is love, sweet love, but I would like to present the opposing view. What the world needs is motorcycles that can turn into helicopters and utterly customizable battle armor beamed from a space station.

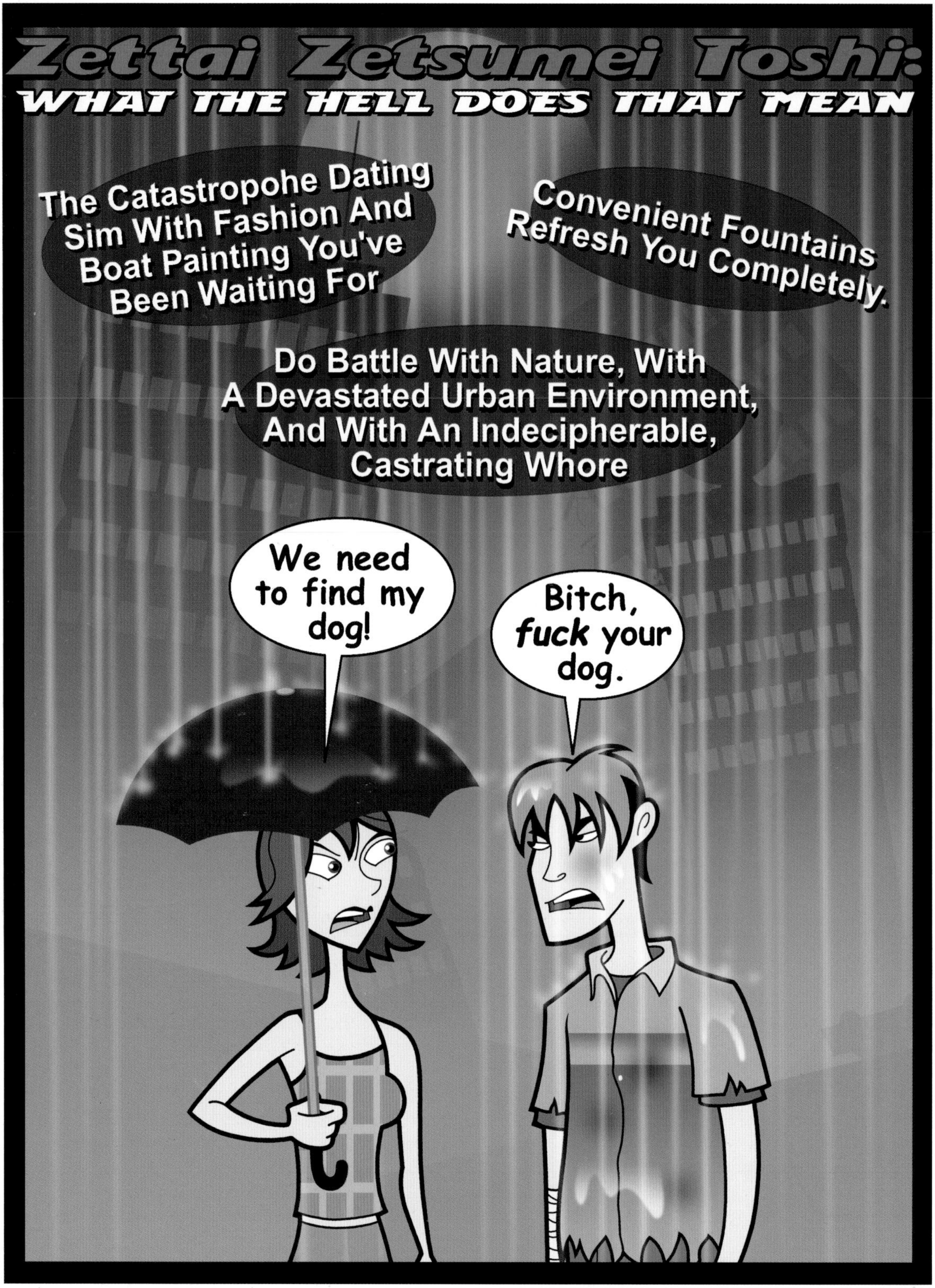
Zettai Zetsumei Toshi:
WHAT THE HELL DOES THAT MEAN
The Catastropohe Dating Sim With Fashion And Boat Painting You've Been Waiting For
Convenient Fountains Refresh You Completely.
Do Battle With Nature, With A Devastated Urban Environment, And With An Indecipherable, Castrating Whore
We need to find my dog!
Bitch, *fuck* your dog.

ZETTA ZITIBITIBADAYAYA

June 17, 2002 Zettai Zetsumei Toshi was ultimately released here as Disaster Report, where it picked up middling reviews. I'm of the opinion that the game is actually a good deal more entertaining when you don't know what's going on—taken as a purely foreign experience—as evidenced by this review of the game which we presented at the time. I rarely write what you would call a long-form, traditional review, so I must have liked it quite a lot.

Although I was hot for the Land of the Rising Fun concept, I've definitely thought of it as a Gabe thing, an excuse to make his Neo fetish a more demonstrable facet of the site, perhaps. Maybe it is an attempt to kill me dead by writing an entire article without using a single comma. Fair enough. Really, anything that keeps him off the street and out of the public eye meets with my most vigorous applause.

The main issue is that he and I prefer different games, and that's the long and the short of it. The action genre he favors is rarely going to be hindered overmuch by the fact that Japanese—as a language—looks like rows of disciplined insects, and not really any kind of language at all. The RPGs and strategy games I crave, on the other hand, would be rendered incomprehensible (by and large) by that fact, and so I'd essentially surrendered interest. And that's when they struck.

The moment we tore into our latest shipment, something was different. Obviously, a hybrid of action and RPG would (quite necessarily) be more streamlined than RPG alone, as the tenets of the stern Action Lords dictate. The new GBA Castlevania, which appears to call itself "Concerto of Midnight Sun," is completely accessible in my opinion—and I don't know a lick of Japanese. Some experimentation is required, yeah, but you'd have to have had a recent head trauma not to grasp this stuff. What's more, it's great. Looks delicious. You will literally see things in the first ten seconds that will surprise you. They've switched out Circle of the Moon's card shit for a new spell system, which, you know, hey. Whatever you need to do, Japan. I'm not really here to talk about Castlevania, but if questions about it start to pop up in my mail I'll gladly do so later. I've got to be honest with you. I've got something else on my mind.

Zettai Zetsumei Toshi is, as I had hoped, fantastic. That's the Playstation 2 game they're calling "survival horror," except with earthquakes and not zombies, but I hardly think this game is a valid application of that nomenclature. For one thing, it has a very heavy platform element: jumping on shit, balancing on other shit, falling off shit to your death. You know what I'm talking about. The combination of mature themes and that kind of gameplay is interesting to see in practice. There's a heavy inventory management angle, which is common to what people call survival horror—but just about the time we're outgrowing one backpack, they give us a new one which has a spacious interior and sleeps four. In fact, the one we have now is like a Goddamn costume trunk or something as well, it's that substantial, and it's filled with hats and sunglasses. I don't even need to tell you how pleased I am about that.

Your objectives are pretty straightforward, namely to escape an artificial island off the coast of Japan after a severe earthquake, and the pacing has been excellent these first six hours. There's more dialogue and text here than in, let's say, a Castlevania, but you're managing a much more complicated scenario than deciding which bat to whip. You'll meet people, emasculating people, people who will take your umbrella and they won't even *care*. I've seen them do it. Maybe this is a problem in Nippon. Highly cinematic, the familiar urban environment you've seen so many times before is now an absolute deathtrap. Don't get used to a building being there because odds are good

you'll be wearing it as a hat here in a minute. The scenery is very dynamic, oft times as gamers we will take solace in the fact that something in an environment is too big to ever possibly move, like the ground, but you can make no such assumptions here. Each level—they aren't labeled as such, but you move from place to place, each with a discrete purpose, and that's called a *level*—involves you needing to help people and get out, while taking every article of clothing you can find and wearing it immediately, even if it doesn't "go." For example, as our shirt and jeans became ever more ragged, we were clearly moving into fashionable territory, and something had to be done. A pair of safety gloves, Ray-Bans with yellow lenses, and a bus driver's hat clearly do not make up a regulation ensemble, but we had a crowbar, so it's not like anybody was going to give us any shit about it. Plus, they're almost all dead.

The game is completely unmodified from its Japanese release, because it *is* the Japanese release, so even outside of me not knowing what the hell these people are talking about I feel like I'm having some kind of cultural exchange. I can't speak to this one in particular, but the story in most games—let alone Japanese ones—isn't really an afterthought, because that implies that they thought about it at all. So, in the absence of any intelligible narrative, we just concoct our own in real time. For us, Zettai Zetsumei Toshi is an allegory for relations between the sexes, and it works especially well at this because we don't speak Japanese. She will say things, and we have no idea what the hell is going on, and then we'll select from a list of responses, but we have no idea which one is the right one, and then they're all wrong. It works on a lot of levels. The crumbling metropolis is your self-determination and capacity to feel any kind of pleasure in this life whatsoever. The puppy you must rescue later symbolizes a stupid little fucker. You're given a chance to go with either a man or a woman later, which I guess might mean they're just going in, you know, different directions but I'm still satisfied with my prior analysis. We navigated a mysterious conversation tree four layers deep, talking to a woman in the pouring rain. This culminated, inexplicably, in her stealing our umbrella, which we blamed Monkey for. She still didn't look very happy, but that's because we hadn't been buried alive in wreckage. And don't think it's because she hasn't been trying.

The level of collectibility and customization in this game is strange, and I don't know if that's more common in Japanese games in general, or what. The multifarious clothing options I've already discussed, but even something like the compass that sits down in the corner of the screen has no less than fifteen different variations you can discover. There was a strange blue canister near us, and we didn't understand exactly what it was used for—until we realized that it was allowing us to try different paint jobs on a boat. It's a very small thing, but the amount of ownership it conferred to us in our own destiny (and the destiny of our ingenious watercraft) was noteworthy.

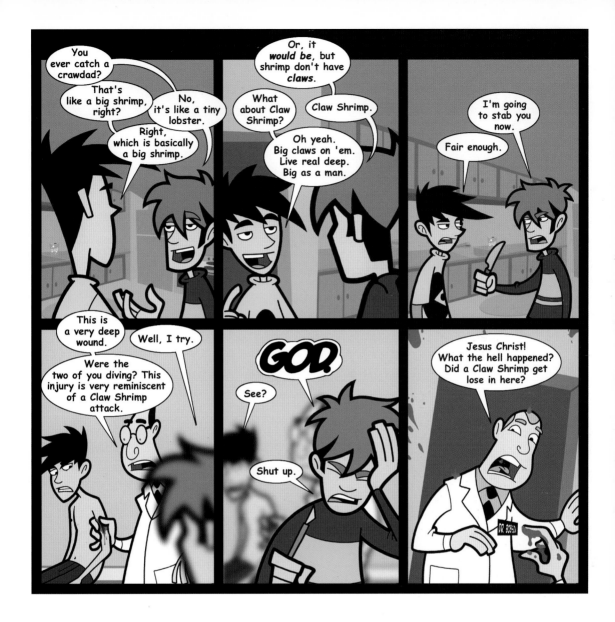

CLAW SHRIMP

June 19, 2002 This comic is, at its core, a relief map that shows the odd contours of our process. It seems strange even to me, and I was there for the duration, but we really did get into a fairly heated argument about what characteristics truly confer "lobster" status. Neither of us are marine biologists—that probably goes without saying, but I feel compelled to establish how devoid of scientific merit this conversation must have been.

It's like when two people start talking about how many words Eskimos have for snow or time, but they aren't linguists, and they don't know any Eskimos, they're just two people talking about nothing for an interminable duration.

SUMMON MONSTER I

June 21, 2002 I will agree that summoning a badger, on the face of it, doesn't seem that cool. But there is a more elaborate version of a badger, called a Dire Badger, and it is not so easily dismissed. These are the badgers they have in hell. A regular badger might growl or eat a truffle. Dire Badgers are bad hombres—they rob banks and double-cross Robert DeNiro. They are almost inexpressibly hardcore.

MY MINORITY REPORT REPORT

June 24, 2002 You need to know this, and right away: there are certain classes of entertainment upon which I cannot be relied upon to give useful answers, because my affection for them is too great. Movies based on Philip K. Dick books are one such class. The others, purely for trivia purposes, are Things with Robots in Them, Artificial Intelligence, and Sherlock Holmes.

SAVED GAMES WITH FATHER WARD

June 26, 2002 The second of these comics was originally a donation gift, but since there are only two Father Ward comics in existence we thought they should probably be together.

We had always wanted to do a cartoon version of a call-in show. For some reason those two things seemed to fit for us, but when we tried to consider the personality behind the microphone we kept going back to the image of a priest. Not just for the heals and buffs: a character devoted to saving souls *and* saving the princess. Every now and then we'll meet the one guy who liked Father Ward at a convention, and we all share a *moment*.

SANITY'S ROQUEFORT

June 28, 2002 Eternal Darkness: Sanity's Requiem has an overwrought title. Luckily, everything else about the game is wrought to exacting specifications. And honestly, as this ancient, epic storyline plays out, over the course of many playable characters conferring with many evil gods, the name of the game starts to feel about right.

CARTRIDGEZZZ

July 1, 2002 Printing out the (ahem) "Internet Web" is not a good ink investment, no. Our moms would be proud, though: just look at us engaging in raucous "visual experiments." The next time an asshole mimics sign language to insult your comprehension, remember that we have transformed the entire process into art. We at Penny Arcade hope that this will provide some comfort.

FEAR

July 3, 2002 THQ was, about this time, hauling some Xbox franchises over to Nintendo's portable. Gabe wouldn't own an Xbox for another month yet, so he still felt some trepidation over this . . . unseemly . . . commingling. I recall that whenever circumstances forced him to hold the Xbox controller, he wore his scowl prominently.

WHAT'S NEXT?

July 5, 2002 We'd just read a story about some kind of evil science goat, where they had somehow gotten some spider DNA lodged into it, so now the goat's milk was full of silk. It's probably scarier to *think* about than it is in practice—picture a hulking, eight-eyed black *goat* in the middle of a web the size of a parachute. We thought about taking this technology and turning it to our own delicious purpose.

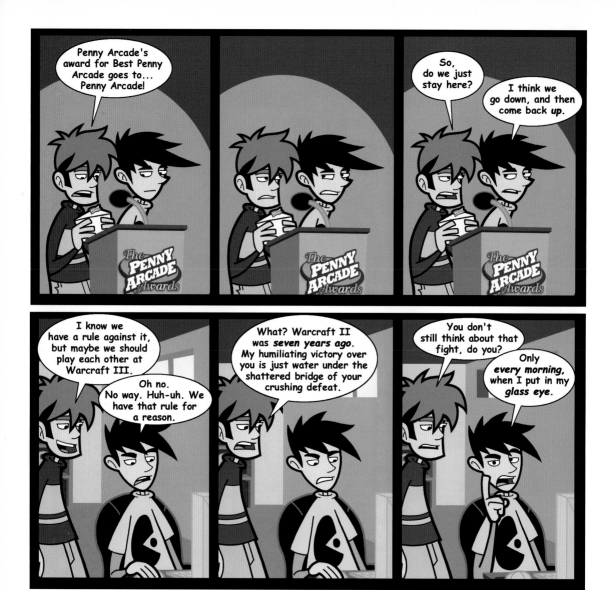

IT'S THE BIG NIGHT

July 8, 2002 In 2002, we asked that the Web Cartoonists' Choice Awards remove our names from the running. It just makes people mad when we're in there, and we don't care if we win. At least, that's what we *thought*. When we saw others heaving *their* beautiful statues, we began to crave that shining weight. Our solution was, I think, *novel*.

SON OF TRUE STORY

July 10, 2002 Outside of fighters or the (very) occasional FPS, Gabriel and I make it a point not to play games against one another. I'm sure I've written about this somewhere else, hopefully not somewhere else in this *book*, but there was a period after an especially vicious round of Duke Nukem 3D where we did not speak for a week. We don't really have that luxury anymore. I have to see that fucker every day.

AROMATIC

July 12, 2002 This was when Apple had that "Switch" bullshit running, which went on to become one of the most aggressively and cleverly pilloried campaigns in existence. Jesus H. Christ. This garbage alone delayed my Mac purchase by probably four years, all by itself.

THE WARCRAFT III ISSUE

July 15, 2002 We played it every, every night. But Gabe played it more than that—saving out his matches, watching them carefully, and taking copious notes. As I've established many times over, as soon as a game becomes some kind of work, I'm out. But it's *got* to become work. It's got to be taken seriously if you want to excel in a multiplayer context. I made my peace with last place a long time ago.

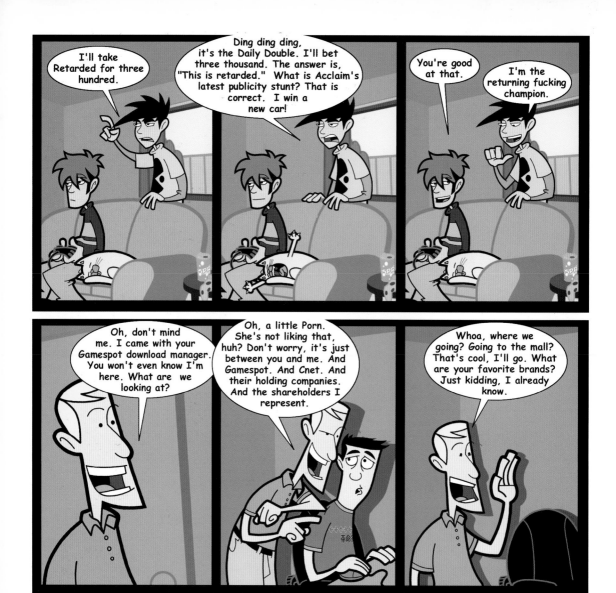

THANKS PAT

July 17, 2002 They're back now, in some evil context, but Acclaim in its heyday was known for the most vile kind of stunts. This comic was in response to their latest maneuver, a shabby thing for a game called Shadowman, where they were offering to advertise the game on people's tombstones. What did they say? These guys were champs. They suggested it might "particularly interest poorer families."

WITH FRIENDS LIKE THESE

July 19, 2002 Gamespot had recently partnered with a company to provide a download manager for the site, and the fear after digging into the EULA and investigating this component was that nasty things were possible. This "feature" eventually "disappeared."

M$

July 22, 2002 I am far more likely to take threats of this kind seriously, but that dollar-sign rhetorical flourish is as foul to me as it is my cohort. There are things in this world that I dislike. One of the things I dislike the most is a serious argument, well constructed, delivered by someone who makes themselves difficult to respect.

THE MODERN ARCADE

July 24, 2002 It was nice getting back into an arcade two or three times a week, meeting people, getting on good terms with the people running it—in other words, going about things much as we had eight years before this comic. The whole thing makes me want to take up my guitar and, while I pick and strum, describe the exact parameters of the Good Old Days.

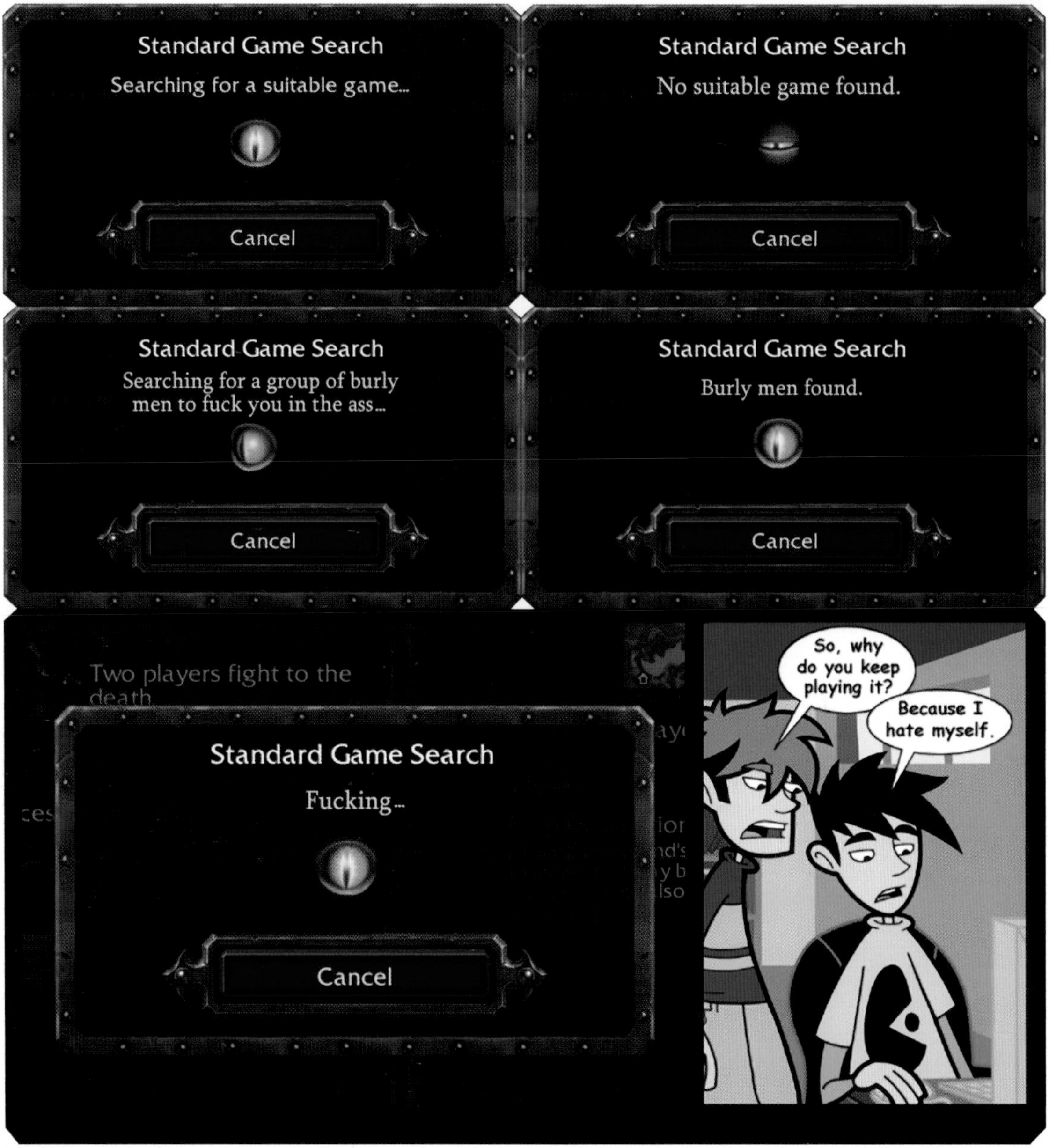
Standard Game Search
Searching for a suitable game...
Cancel
Standard Game Search
No suitable game found.
Cancel
Standard Game Search
Searching for a group of burly men to fuck you in the ass...
Cancel
Standard Game Search
Burly men found.
Cancel
Two players fight to the death
Standard Game Search
Fucking...
Cancel
So, why do you keep playing it?
Because I hate myself.

MAKE ME A MATCH

July 26, 2002 On the web, this comic is actually animated, and that cool eye is looking all around. *Very* fancy. At the time, I included a short guide to help people lose more efficiently—to lose, in effect, the *Penny Arcade Way*. It is with great pleasure that I present this ancient wisdom, long lost to man.

Warcraft III is the game of choice around here, as I am sure it is elsewhere, and we lose virtually every time we play online. It's actually sort of a joke now—asking someone if they want to "lose at Warcraft" is essentially inviting them to play at all—but we don't really mind it. The fact is that we are better at losing than most, we can be defeated more spectacularly and in less time than most, and we can *parlay* our strong chain of early successes into fiery perdition. Like the young man who blames the controller, or the Brenna who blames the Dance Dance pad, we carry on the rich tradition of blaming the mechanism for our own ineptitude. As I said, it's no big deal. When you're as good at losing as we are, you're really a part of the winning team anyhow, working together with your captor to ensure that his stay in your base is a pleasant one, and ensuring repeat business from his ravening and rapacious horde. How do we do it? It's easy:

Don't Build Defenses of Any Kind, as these will only impede their grave Taurens in the performance of their duty, which is pulverizing your entire Goddamn operation. Instead, furnish your foes with quenching potables such as branded sports drinks to help them regain lost electrolytes. Remember, your annihilation is thirsty work. Be grateful for his attention!

Never Build Units That Can Attack Air, because they may inadvertently destroy enemy air units. Why not build mainly first-tier combatants, like Grunts, Huntresses, Footmen, and Ghouls? When Undead Frost Wyrms breathe gusts of frigid corpse breath, it is your obligation to die. But, please make a show of running to and fro, as the dance of prey will often excite and entice your master while he floats on the wind.

Try Not To Expand, because your moral and intellectual superior on the other end of the Battle.net desperately needs that cash if he is to produce the most fabulous units the game has to offer. You may gaze upon his unholy Abominations, powerful Gryphons, and leathery Chimaera with a sense of real pride, knowing that you helped make it all possible.

If you act in accordance with our Three Ways of Failure, we guarantee that—as early as your first game—you will experience a reaming so intense that you will wonder if anything you felt up to this point was real.

A GRAVE ISSUE

July 29, 2002 To this day, 'round the middle of summer, Gabe starts to get an itch for Super Mario Sunshine. I seem to recall it being received by our population in an uneven way, its additions to the formula not being universally adored. I don't find this particularly odd, as the game is weird as shit. But I would say that we experienced it under perhaps optimal circumstances, as a kind of spectator sport, where fabulous platforming tricks met with midair spray gun acrobatics in a way that entertained the entire room.

That is how we've always played games, indeed, that dynamic is the basis of our partnership, the comics it produces, and the books that collect them. Even single player games, in this reckoning, become multiplayer experiences. Shameful performances are ridiculed. Controllers are swapped during difficult portions. And you may be assured, sir or madam, that pizzas are *ordered*.

Super Mario Galaxy, I would assert, retains that mysterious quantity, *wonder*, which characterizes this strange plumber and his endless travails.

GRIPPING!

July 31, 2002 It was our plan to go to Japan, actually and for real, and I think we had completed all the very highest levels of planning without securing the green foundation that *realizes* such endeavors. We have to go eventually—like E3, Japan represents for our people a *holy* site. But if you'd never looked at what it costs to fly and stay there, assuming that those vast numbers are even recognizable to you, it may be that you find yourself *short of breath*.

TA-DAAAA

August 2, 2002 We are nothing if not compliant. It was Gabe's intention to try and make this comic entirely on Kiko's Macintosh as a kind of experiment, but before he was even halfway done he quit in frustration and returned to the PC across the room. He owns two Macs now, but he still doesn't do anything on them you would call *work*.

I KNOW YOU ARE

August 5, 2002 This conversation is not atypical. Schoolyard combat of this kind characterized many of these interactions. Victory was usually determined by the first mom defiled. I don't think we are especially proud of this.

I'LL FORM THE ETC.

August 7, 2002 Now, with the power of future vision, we know just how early all of this Playstation 3 discussion actually was. By the time you read this book, of course, you may also be a PS3 owner—you'll know things about it, perhaps amazing things, which this past version of me isn't aware of. But it's become clear, over the last couple years especially, that Sony has been kind of making it up as they go along.

I'M SORRY

August 9, 2002 First of all, *no*, Gabriel's art did not improve significantly between the last comic and this one. The work before you is the work of my own hand. See how each color is perfectly placed? In my pieces, there are no accidents. Like Athena, each one springs from my mind fully formed.

As to the subject matter, something very much like what we described here became a reality with Starcraft Ghost. And then, after a few prominent E3 showings, it evaporated. That's the only word that accurately describes what happened. It was a physical thing, and then it boiled away to nothing and disappeared.

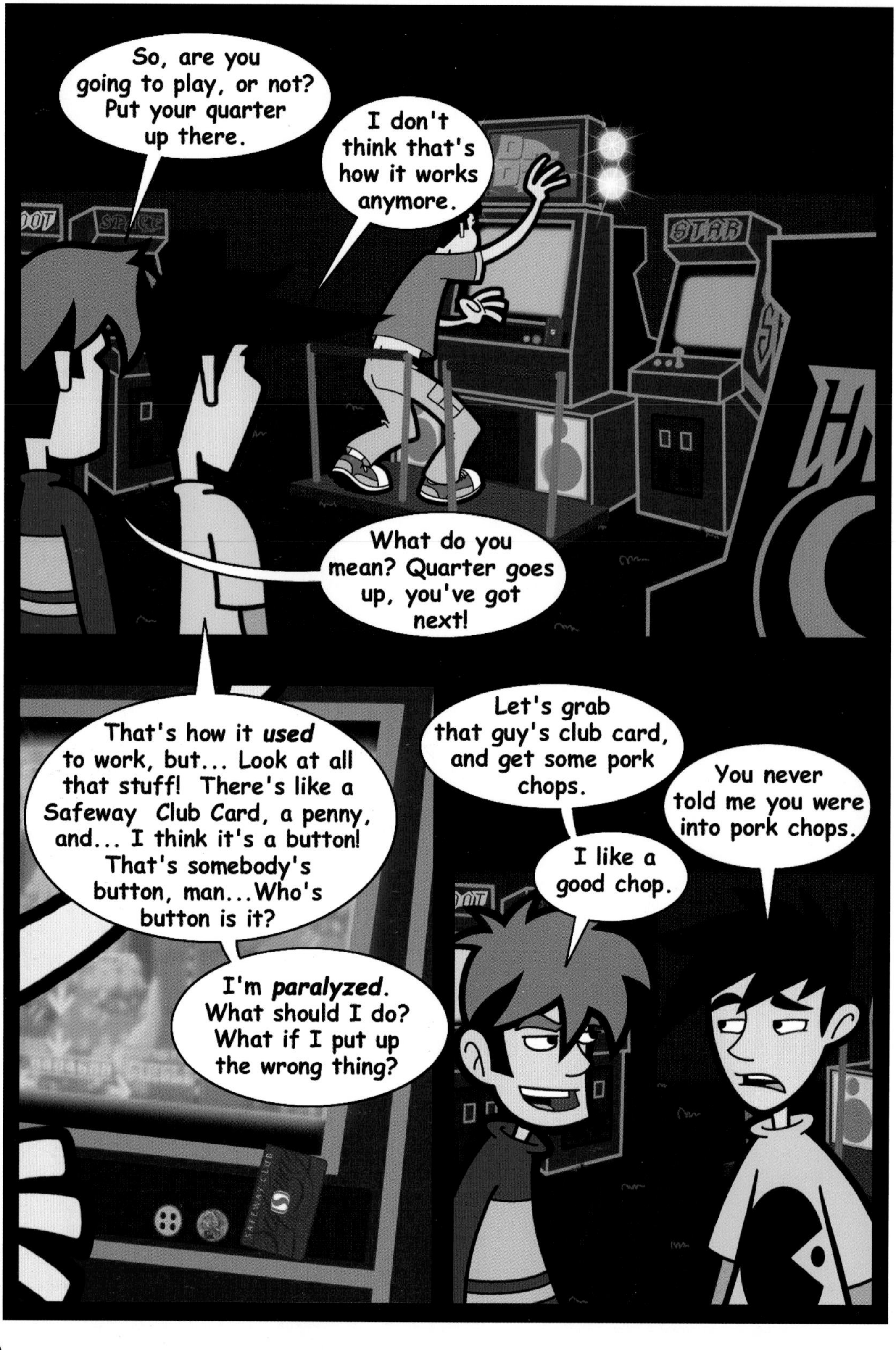
So, are you going to play, or not? Put your quarter up there.
I don't think that's how it works anymore.
What do you mean? Quarter goes up, you've got next!
That's how it *used* to work, but... Look at all that stuff! There's like a Safeway Club Card, a penny, and... I think it's a button! That's somebody's button, man...Who's button is it?
I'm *paralyzed*. What should I do? What if I put up the wrong thing?
Let's grab that guy's club card, and get some pork chops.
You never told me you were into pork chops.
I like a good chop.
SAFEWAY CLUB

OUR DIRTY SECRET

August 12, 2002 By this time, our unfashionable addiction to Dance Dance Revolution—in flagrant disregard of the Unified Hardcore Gamer Code (UHGC)—was something we could no longer keep off the front page. DDR has its own social culture, a fact we were not aware of, playing the game mostly in the basement where we play the rest of our games. Read the following for a tale of game enthusiasts plucked from security and thrust into contact with their species:

Our recent arcade experience was absolutely *bewildering*.

It's not news that we get down on occasion, or perhaps even fall down and hurt ourselves. But the place we typically do these things at has enough machines so that there really isn't any question about who goes next. There's the people on there dance dancing, and then there's two other people with one foot already on the pad waiting to go. The only time there's any confusion is when the line itself actually stretches around the entire planet Earth.

This isn't what you get at a smaller arcade.

There were these five guys at the arcade we stopped at who were clearly in the throes of some kind of addiction, and I can't be sure that it was an addiction to DDR. They had wild, malarial eyes and seemed haunted by unseen forces. Any time they were not in contact with the (apparently quite invigorating) dance pads, they shambled about in a vaguely funky throng reminiscent of Michael Jackson's "Thriller." It was time to get mine, clearly, and show these undead motherfuckers how the PA crew does it on the *easiest level*. I stepped forward, gleaming Georgia quarter in hand, prepared to place it in the silver procession of succession that exists on every arcade cabinet.

Does anybody know when people just started putting any old Goddamn thing up on the machine?

This is one of the more sensible mechanisms of arcade etiquette, in my opinion. You take a quarter, and you put it on the Goddamn *thing*. That's where it goes. Then, *you* can go. Get it? No buttons, no *pennies*, and sure as *shit* no Safeway Club Cards. Some fucker put his Health Insurance card up there, but in his defense I don't think he actually knew where he was. It's possible he just came in for a checkup. But these other mongrels, they knew exactly what they were doing. We stood back from the machine, demonstrably freaked out by this random parade of items—like a criminal line-up in some pocket *society*. I didn't know what the hell all that stuff up there meant. So, I empty out my *own* pocket on there, figuring that at least *one* of the things in there would secure me a spot. I put up a quarter, you know, and, just in case, a dime, a penny, two nickels, another quarter, and a stick of Wrigley's Doublemint Gum. When the guy got done with his songs, he looked at my stuff, then he looked over at me, then he looked at my stuff, and back to me again. He did this for five minutes. I shrugged. "Yeah," I said. "I don't really know what's going on."

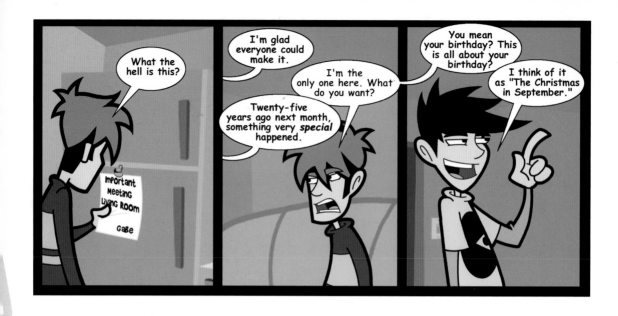

MEIN BIRTHDAY

August 14, 2002 You might *also* have a friend who believes that he is the Son of God every time that cursed date appears. Where does this behavior come from? Where does it begin? I can imagine him in a tiny cape, the tyrant as a young man, issuing orders of various kinds from the end of some makeshift scepter.

His appetite for increasingly elaborate gifts has made it necessary for everyone who knows him to "gang up" in order to purchase them, as they are beyond the reach of mortal finances. You may be interested to know how it's shaken out the last few years:

2002 Some Real Unicorns
2003 Ludacris
2004 One (1) Mummy
2005 A Huge Pile Of "Fucking Gold"
2006 The "Red" Lion (From Voltron)

I'M UP

August 16, 2002 Recently, Gabriel made enemies. As he is always making enemies, one must take careful notes in order to monitor each feud as it takes the stage and then sheepishly recedes. I've been using Microsoft Excel to keep track of them. It's been an improvement.

This time it was because he said that Will Wright's Spore wasn't actually a game. He didn't mean to be offensive when he said it, but offending people is his superpower. He thinks that it's more of a toolkit for creating your own games, with your own objectives, which is something he would distinguish from games in the classic sense. It's not really that controversial. He's essentially saying that hammers and saws aren't houses, assertions to which any reasonable person would agree.

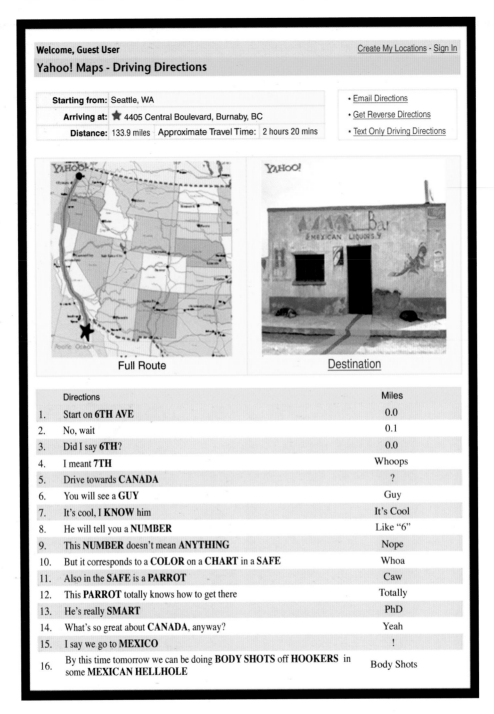

Create My Locations - Sign In

Yahoo! Maps - Driving Directions

Starting from:	Seattle, WA
Arriving at:	⭐ 4405 Central Boulevard, Burnaby, BC
Distance: 133.9 miles	**Approximate Travel Time:** 2 hours 20 mins

- Email Directions
- Get Reverse Directions
- Text Only Driving Directions

Full Route | Destination

	Directions	Miles
1.	Start on **6TH AVE**	0.0
2.	No, wait	0.1
3.	Did I say **6TH**?	0.0
4.	I meant **7TH**	Whoops
5.	Drive towards **CANADA**	?
6.	You will see a **GUY**	Guy
7.	It's cool, **I KNOW** him	It's Cool
8.	He will tell you a **NUMBER**	Like "6"
9.	This **NUMBER** doesn't mean **ANYTHING**	Nope
10.	But it corresponds to a **COLOR** on a **CHART** in a **SAFE**	Whoa
11.	Also in the **SAFE** is a **PARROT**	Caw
12.	This **PARROT** totally knows how to get there	Totally
13.	He's really **SMART**	PhD
14.	What's so great about **CANADA**, anyway?	Yeah
15.	I say we go to **MEXICO**	!
16.	By this time tomorrow we can be doing **BODY SHOTS** off **HOOKERS** in some **MEXICAN HELLHOLE**	Body Shots

CAN YOU TELL ME HOW TO GET

August 19, 2002 I don't know if online map services have improved since then, but we got a number of truly psychotic driving suggestions to that year's Necrowombicon event. One of the destinations was underwater, a thousand miles off the east coast of the United States. Another of their famous purple lines directed us into the mouth of Kilauea, an active Hawaiian volcano.

DESCENT

August 21, 2002 One learned quickly to use the "nine" key, though it was far away from the customary input clusters, but it seemed like a Public Service Announcement might be in order. We received a mail from one of the developers after this comic was released, declaring that this was a purposeful decision designed to separate the men from the (presumably shattered) boys.

OUT BACK

August 26, 2002 We sat on the floor, slowly rocking back and forth, waiting for the new Transformers series to begin. When it did begin, and it was monstrous on the face of it, we responded in the traditional format. I won't rewrite history and say that the cartoons we watched as young men weren't marketing platforms, but at least in our shows the characters *themselves* were not obsessed with collecting the Goddamn toys.

BEHIND THE SUNSHINE

August 28, 2002 The emotional, physical, and spiritual "high" one receives from grasping Super Mario Sunshine's stars (or "shines") is powerful enough to make one fall from the couch and shudder in their extremities. Our meditations on the shine lifestyle and where it must inexorably lead inspired this brave work, which we hope will show young people the dangers associated with these unbelievably pleasurable substances.

SO, COM?

August 30, 2002 On the PC side of things, voice chat is primarily used by friends to communicate with other friends. When one jumps into *unregulated chat* with a radically different group of people, one really does hear some *remarkable phrases*.

UNWISDOM

September 2, 2002 You might notice that I am naked in this strip, wrapped only in a blanket. From that day's post: "It is a true story, even if it was him in the blanket and him who got in trouble. Also, it was a different game and I was wearing a chef's hat. We were ass-deep in iguanas during this period, and I was seriously considering becoming a beekeeper."

FANTASTIC

September 4, 2002 There was a place called Roasters down the street from the spider's nest he was living in then, and sometimes (just to escape it, I think) he would trudge down and eat a Thanksgiving meal—far out of that food's traditional season. He knew he could be fatally bitten at any minute, which made every day a kind of celebration.

OF TRAILERS

September 6, 2002 Powerful, *powerful* metaphor. I'm actually afraid to say anything else, lest some of that extraordinary power be lost.

BLADE'S BLIND DATE

September 9, 2002 The problem these days is that when you meet someone for the first time, you don't really know where they stand on the issues of the day. Is she into *vampire rights*? You don't know. You *don't know!* You need to stick to innocuous shit, like . . . What did Bob say? Photos. Something about *photos*.

IKARUGA

September 11, 2002 There was never a chance that I wasn't going to love Ikaruga—it's a genre I'm genetically predisposed to. That it was also *excellent* didn't hurt, and that you can . . . Well, I have a bunch of room over there on the next page. I'll go into it there. We did just dig it back out again, though. It held up *strong*.

MORE IKARUGA

September 13, 2002 Did I mention that the game was also co-operative? That's us there on the couch, proving it. The best shooters of this kind do have this feature, of course, but this is a game where it really feels critical. I'm talking about it like you haven't played it. You probably have, I know that deep down, but I sometimes feel like the books are an opportunity to record game history. I apologize.

Ikaruga is a *shmup*—a "shoot-them-up," sometimes also known as a "space shooter." As a primarily arcade genre, it's old as the hills. And this one in particular is by an outfit called Treasure, which has a real handle on the form.

Just as in Raiden, or Alcon (or Xevious . . .), you are tasked with rocking motherfuckers as the screen crawls up. Avoiding complex patterns of bullets is a staple in this type of game, but the hook in Ikaruga is that your ship can change its "polarity" from light to dark (or vice versa) and absorb shots of that color. It adds an almost platform flavor to an already satisfying experience, because now that you have another means to avoid this ordnance they feel comfortable cooking up some pretty sophisticated traps. It came out on the Cube eventually, but, I mean, *come on*. This will always be a Dreamcast game.

THE NEW CRAZE

September 16, 2002 Unreal Tournament 2003 included a gametype new to the series entitled "Bombing Run." It was at the nexus of so many of my gameplay fantasies that sometimes I would just laugh out loud while playing it. It's like basketball with rocket launchers, essentially. Or maybe Capture the Flag, where you can shoot the flag through a goal. Anyway, it was great.

TM(™)

September 18, 2002 This is only going to get more intense as development costs rise. But there is another factor in its inevitability, and those with some spiritual sensitivity may be aware of the source: a freak celestial conflux called "The Blood Eye" is, with every passing year, bringing Hell itself closer to the Earth.

THE OTHER KIND OF GHOST

September 20, 2002 Nihilistic worked on Starcraft: Ghost for a time anyway, and then some other guys worked on it, and then those other guys got bought, or abducted by aliens, or *something*. Much of the story is unknown, but it is rumored that, for whatever reason, the teams that work on Starcraft: Ghost just keep dying.

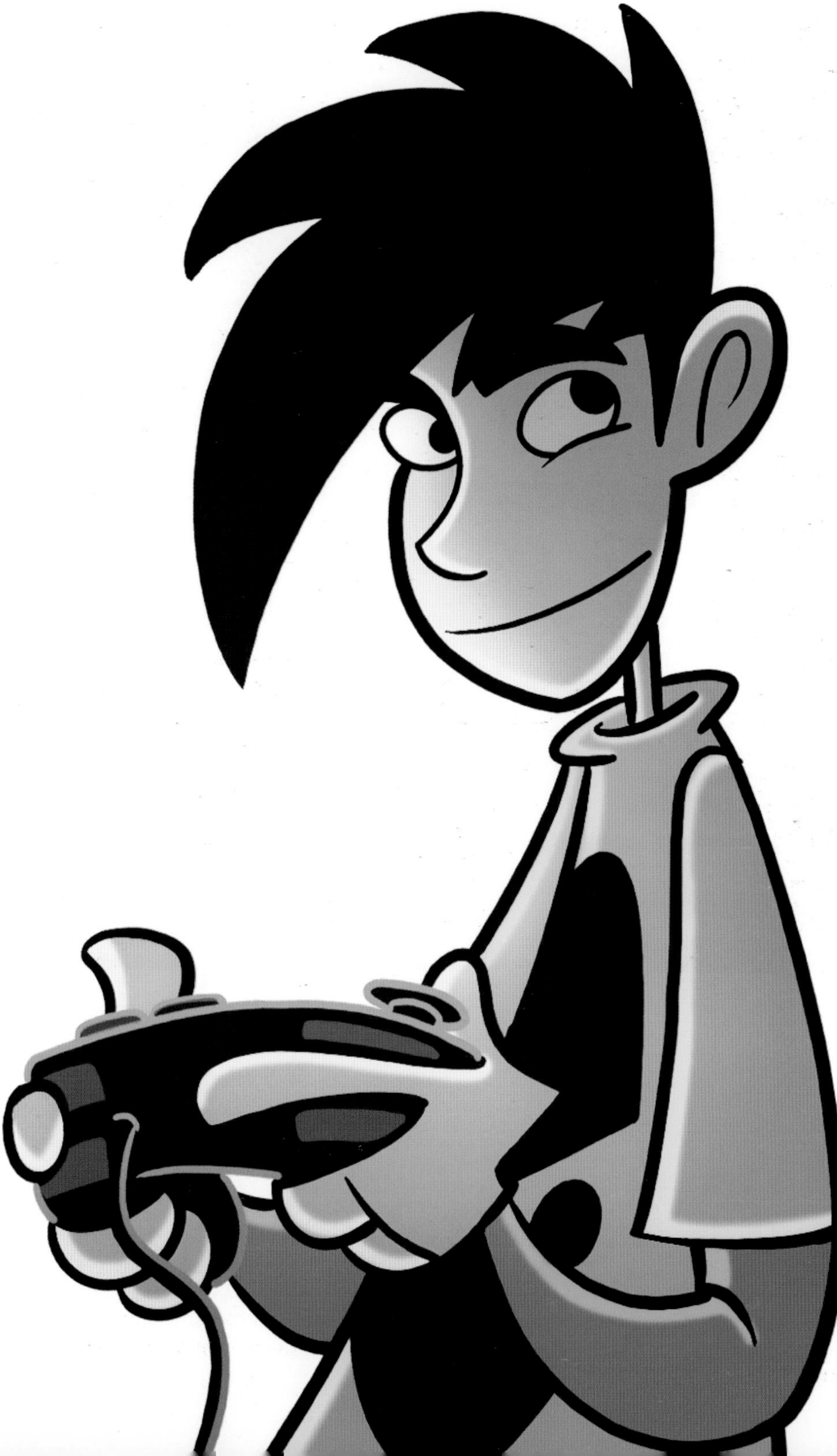

SHUT UP

September 23, 2002 You've got the wars that break out between individual consoles. That's always sort of going on, people carrying the banner of a console years in advance of its release to secure their place in Sony heaven.

But click it one level of magnification back, and you can see that there is another conflict with stakes so high that the supporters of those disparate systems will join ranks to turn out the foe: the vile and treacherous *PC gamer*.

(CONTINUED)

Having only gotten into consoles seriously in 2000 or so, I don't know enough about the console *mindset* to communicate its position with any elegance. I can tell you that the average PC gamer sees even the grip of the console enthusiast upon the controller as cause for disgust and alarm. There is something stunted about it, in an evolutionary sense. Compared to the elegant, versatile keyboard and mouse, this *devotion* to their hideous little idols is debased and perhaps even a kind of sin.

THIS EXPLAINS A LOT

September 25, 2002 Rare kicked out monstrous, warmed-over, back-burner product for Microsoft's Xbox and then, with great strain, hunkered down over a pile of newspapers and "produced" Perfect Dark Zero. I was very unhappy for a long time, until I saw what they were doing with Viva Piñata. Probably not going to watch the cartoon. But digging around in a supernatural garden? The odds are pretty good.

MAY NOT BE SPELLED CORRECTLY

September 27, 2002 After watching Gabe play this game for a while, I couldn't believe he was persisting in it. It would have driven me out of my mind—further out of my mind, one might say. It was one hundred percent chore-boy bullshit with only the lightest impetus. It had some cool fur, but I mean, come on. Cats have fur too, just go fucking look at one if you like fur so much.

THOSE GODDAMN CONTAINERS

September 30, 2002 For Christmas, Brenna and I got a set of cordless phones. It took almost twenty minutes of constant work—like miners would work, with precision and tools designed expressly for the purpose—just to penetrate the Goddamn shield around these things. I read later that the package won some kind of award that year for being really hard to open. Man, they weren't fucking kidding.

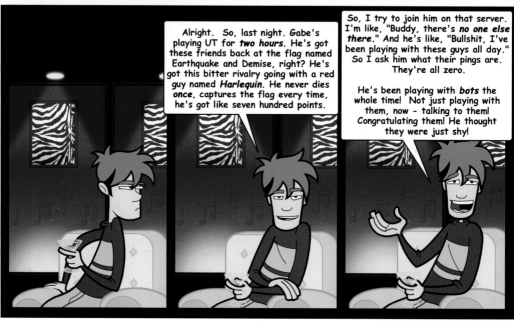

THE REALITY

October 2, 2002 The FairPlay campaign's goal was, essentially, to cut the price of videogames in half. Something that might interest the FairPlay people, wherever they are: Nintendo President Satoru Iwata basically agrees. He thinks that if you're just going to lower the price later, why not make it more affordable from the beginning?

I SWEAR TO GOD

October 4, 2002 This was really embarrassing to him at the time, but eventually he would come to crave the company of bots *exclusively* in his Unreal Tournament games. Apparently his "friends" made quite the impression.

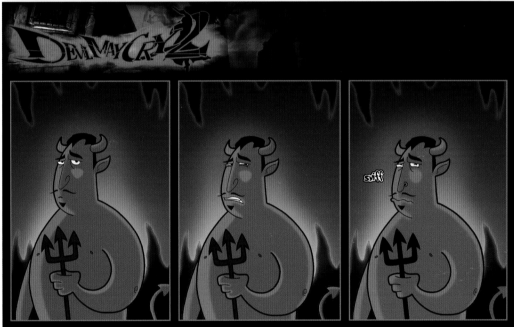

EVERYONE ELSE SEEMS TO LIKE IT

October 7, 2002 Looking back over his thoughts at the time, he implies that the name of the game should perhaps have been changed to "Lame Jumping Puzzles with World's Most Fucked Up Camera Hearts." Whatever deficiencies it must have possessed, apparently the sequel did not bear them. As I recall, he actually had a special version of the strategy guide that included a sticker book. When you met your favorite Disney characters you were supposed to put each sticker on a special page. He did this for more than seventy hours.

WELL, HE MIGHT

October 9, 2002 This one might be, um . . . a little too "high concept."

WE'RE HERE TO HELP

October 11, 2002 Ah, Mr. Period. This strip was meant to target forums in general, but it was the little threads on the EB Games site specifically whose *high* levels of insanity and generally *low* levels of human virtue cried out for comment. These young men really do go "buck wild" upon connecting to the Internet. I think that they might believe they are running some kind of pirate radio station, far from The Man's regulating influence.

ABSOLUTELY RIDICULOUS

October 14, 2002 Remember those crazy fucking guys who converted a car into a mobile sniping platform? You might not recall that (via some highly questionable linkages) they tried to connect games—specifically, those who play them—to this profound tragedy. Gabe wasn't buying into my equally plausible "Sniper Gypsy" hypothesis, but my second Birthday Coupon forced the issue.

ALMOST TRUE

October 16, 2002 When I say Almost True, as I suggested when I named the strip, what I meant was that these events are absolutely true in every way. We attached ourselves bodily to their feeding trough, like Greenpeace activists might secure themselves to a great sequoia, and it was only through ingenuity, luck, and the focused heat of an acetylene cutting torch that we were ever removed.

NOW YOU KNOW

October 18, 2002 Before a wave of dark, sharp karma washed in to scrape Acclaim from the face of the planet, they had gotten it into their heads to make an M rated bicycle trick game. For some reason. We could not generate between us a plausible rationale for this product, thinking instead that they had taken someone's "comment card funnies" as a serious business proposal.

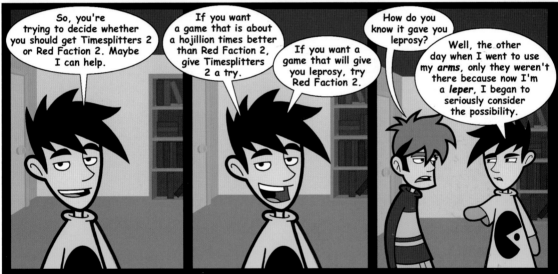

THE SCENT OF FEAR

October 21, 2002 I'm not very good at watching scary movies, being entertained by them, and then pushing them from my mind so that I can resume a normal existence. Part of me has always just *partnered*, in a way, with the media I consume. It's no different with games—but games *typically* don't keep me awake *all night*, my entire body taut with fear.

WINTER BUYING GUIDE

October 23, 2002 Timesplitters 2 amounted to so much raw fun that I really didn't envy the forlorn games that peered up from the retail shelf, so like the sad puppies in the pet store. It's cooperative, which is already worth a lot of points, but there is a "Wild West" themed level in which one player must bust the other out of the county jail! You don't do that shit in Red Faction 1 *or* 2, that's all I'm saying.

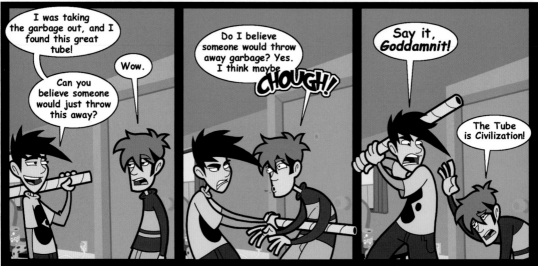

THE NEXT COMIC

October 25, 2002 I called this one "The Next Comic" because, really, what the fuck else do you call it?

I HAVE NO COMMENT

October 30, 2002 It's strange to think that this comic—which is one hundred percent actually about him hitting me with garbage—would morph into such a fixture on the site.

It makes me wonder how much actual control we have over the things we produce, or if we are receiving some kind of signal, extraterrestrial in origin, which bends our will and makes slaves of us. Because rationally, rationally now, I can't connect this strip to extended samurai epics. We did, and continue to do so, but if it seemed like a surprising maneuver to you I need to assert that you and I are surprised together.

GABE IS ANGRY AGAIN

October 28, 2002 This strip made us enemies over there, I'm told. The story as I know it goes like this: Robert met a producer over there on some kind of trip, introduced himself, and upon finding that Gabriel and I were his loathsome paymasters the man launched into a lengthy tirade, which culminated with the statement "I will do everything in my power to be an obstacle to you."

GEIBU

November 1, 2002 Ah, I see. This is where it started to go *nuts*.

BASICALLY TRUE

November 4, 2002 I haven't resorted to peer-to-peer apps outside of BitTorrent for a while, because the signal to noise ratio in those nasty little warrens is way, way out of whack. For every accidental treasure trove like that shown above, the rest is gigs of fake files and corrupt data. Seriously, it's enough to make a person buy an album through legitimate channels!

THE MONEY PROBLEM

November 6, 2002 Steel Battalion, as you might recall, was a Big Robot Sim with a gigantic, three part custom controller that clocked in at two hundred standard Earth dollars. It's ridiculous on the face of it, but as a people who are deeply ridiculous ourselves, something about it *resonated*. Trading in a few recent releases apiece, we came out of there more or less unscathed. I warned you already, I have a diagnosed *Robot Problem*.

AND IN THIS CORNER

November 8, 2002 And now Raiden's all back now, but he's some kind of Ninja Bad-Ass, Gear killer guy. I wish I could play these new ones and enjoy them, but I'm either too smart or too dumb, and I can't figure out which.

TYCHO, MD

November 11, 2002 I've known him for a long time, so I have experience in these matters. He doesn't have a normal stomach, like people do. He has some kind of trap down there that is more like a Food Purgatory. This allows him to maintain an inadvisable diet that causes his body to shut down from time to time. Robert had given him two hundred and fifty-six bottles of Sprite for the aforementioned Christmas in September, and it turns out that man cannot live on Sprite alone. At least, not for more than a couple months.

DISCOURSE

November 13, 2002 Metroid Prime does something that has a tremendous effect on me, but I don't know if my mind is exaggerating the effects, or my willingness to "partner" with entertainment (as described in an earlier entry) is creating it. Explosions and large blasts create flashes of light that cause the character—in the first-person—to be reflected inside the visor. It's a woman's face. Seeing a face reflected in the visor that is not my own, and is, indeed, the *opposite gender*, is one of the most strangely immersive things I've ever seen in a game.

ROYALTAY

November 15, 2002 This "Mech King" appellation is not a made-up thing. I don't know if you can coronate *yourself.* I'm almost sure this must be done by some outside agency, but when he would play the original MechAssault he would often refer to himself with this grand term. He quickly earned a reputation as a mean-spirited and imperious competitor, but that wasn't anything I didn't know already.

IT REALLY IS TERRIBLE

November 18, 2002 Voice support on the original Xbox included a series of voice "masks" that you could apply, Robot and Dark Master being a couple of them. I think they were partly designed to make the user anonymous, but in a closed system where everyone is associated with a unique user name, it serves only to let people annoy the ever-living shit out of each other.

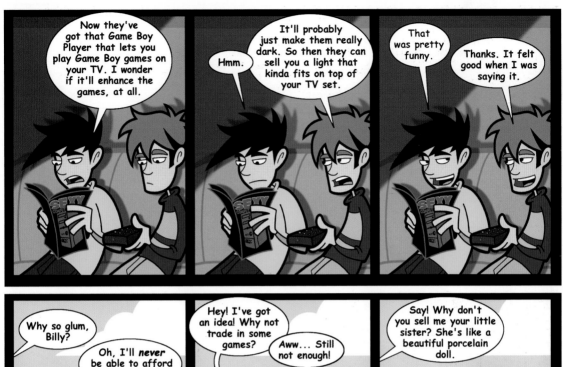

SOMETHING ELSE TO BUY

November 20, 2002 The Game Boy Player was actually a pretty cool device, especially for games you were going to play for long durations—I'm thinking specifically of Tactics Ogre and Final Fantasy Tactics Advance. But they weren't going to score any easy points from us after that GBA shit. It's hard to believe how many just straight-up nasty lighting solutions I put up with before cutting into my machine.

AN EXCELLENT QUESTION

November 22, 2002 There are so many strange, disembodied voices that give advice to young people. It's just considered this accepted thing. I think that if some voice started coming out of nowhere offering me solutions for my problems, I would talk to a doctor and get a prescription of some kind.

A MEDIATION ON VALUE

November 25, 2002 In the same way that an inmate might get a taste for an ingenious "hooch" made from discarded potato peelings, while Gabriel was working at a home electronics store he began to get a taste for the super fancy cables they sold there—those Goddamn Monster Cables. Clocking in at over a hundred dollars an inch, they . . . Well, I guess we did do a comic on it.

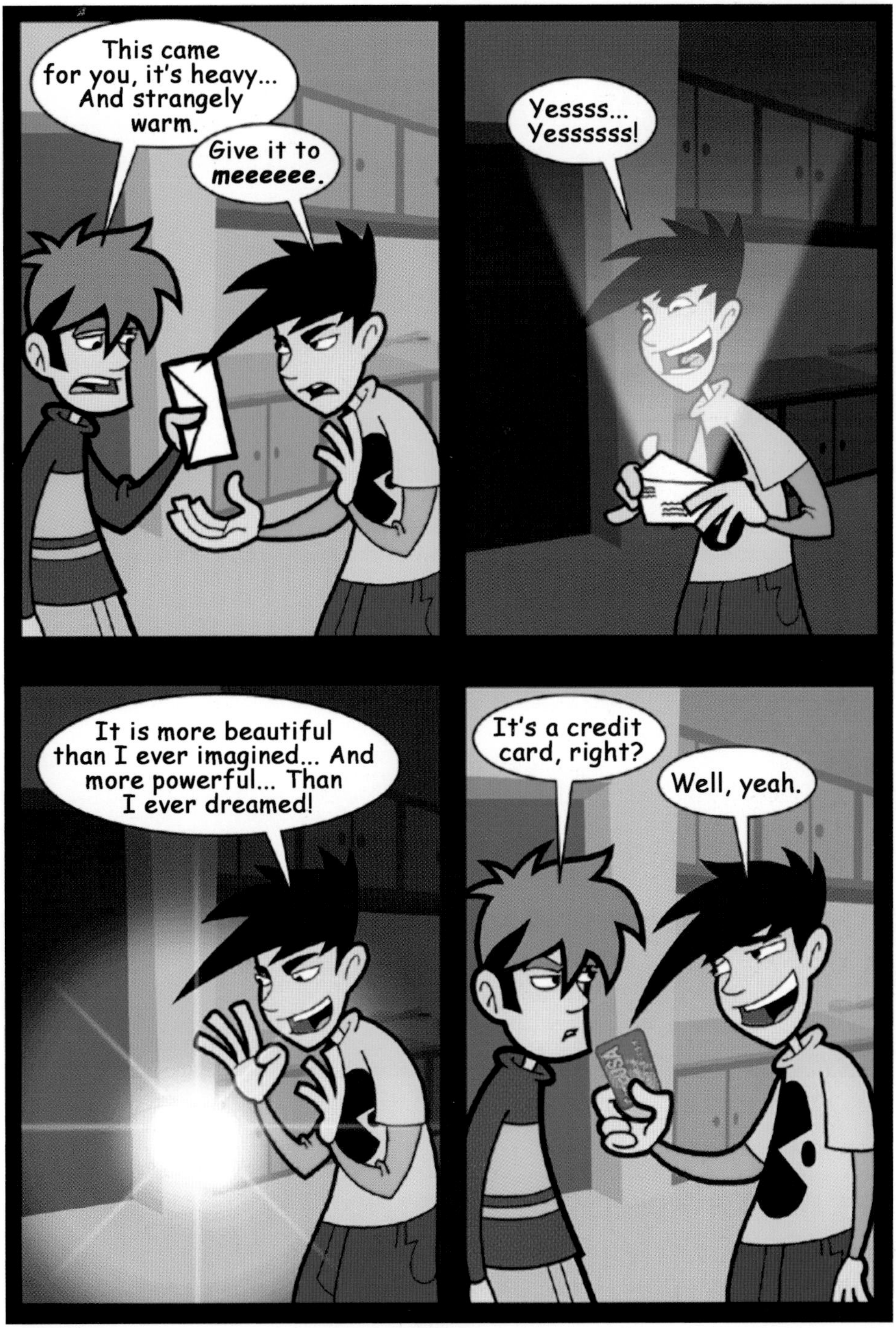
This came for you, it's heavy... And strangely warm.
Give it to meeeeee.
Yessss... Yesssssss!
It is more beautiful than I ever imagined... And more powerful... Than I ever dreamed!
It's a credit card, right?
Well, yeah.

ALSO THE DEVIL'S WORKSHOP, PART ONE

November 27, 2002 I cautioned him against it, as I had once run aground on those reefs myself—but CompUSA's cavern of glittering treasures called to him, like that shit in Aladdin, and he would from time to time push a mine cart heaped with videocards out of that evil hole.

ALSO THE DEVIL'S WORKSHOP, PART TWO

November 29, 2002 He wasn't actually denied. It would be better if he had. There's a lot about the situation I shouldn't discuss. Let me emphasize in the strongest terms that it is a *good thing* we do all of our work under pseudonyms.

HOME IMPROVEMENT

December 2, 2002 Around this time, both the actual Gabriel and the Gabriel that exists in simulation began to take up tools of various kinds and alter their surroundings. Before his amazing metamorphosis, I guess I'd always thought of the Geeky Domains as somewhat ethereal.

LOCATION, LOCATION, LOCATION

December 4, 2002 The sequel to MechAssault, which spurned convention by calling itself *MechAssault 2*, was not a game that really stuck with us. We gave it a couple nights, and then he and I retreated to whatever the game of the month was at that time.

The same could not be said for its predecessor.

I thought I played it a lot, every night a lot, even with the sometimes odd lobby behavior and the growing pains associated with the debut of Microsoft's recently launched Live online service. But Gabe got on before I did, and left sometimes hours after. His Friends List was populated top to bottom with men who could be relied upon to kill with little to no provocation.

River City was only one channel for his mounting aggression, a torrent too vast for a single map to contain. This hatred for the omnipresent foe—an organization calling itself the "Red Team"—would soon spill into the Coliseum, and from there into the Junkyard.

I really did lose him to this game, he dropped off the radar in a way that he wouldn't do again until World of Warcraft. He got out of WoW eventually, too—just in time for the Burning Crusade expansion to haul him back down beneath the waves.

WE'RE PLAYING ASHERON'S CALL 2

December 6, 2002 I tried to suck as much enjoyment and camaraderie as I could out of those times, because I knew he wasn't long for those shores. No MMO ever held him in its grip until World of Warcraft, and I left that game of my own free will and with a song in my heart. Irony of ironies.

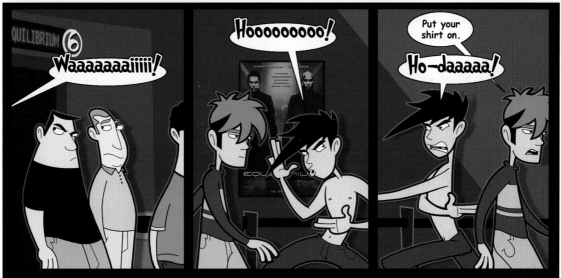

PURE JOY

December 9, 2002 I'm sure that there's something very wrong with us, but if you are some jack-ass and you douse yourself in some kind of elk musk and then run around in the woods until you attract an elk—the raw *purpose* of that substance—and then he leaps upon you in an amorous way, well, it's not something that is going to keep me up at night.

EQUILIBRIUM

December 11, 2002 I remember really liking this movie. It was this sort of crazy mash-up of *The Matrix* and *1984*. This far out, I'm wondering if I really did like it or if I simply liked it more than I expected. I like *liking* it so much that I've been afraid to watch it again.

THE (PRODUCT) CYCLE

December 13, 2002 A little rumor bird told us that there was a new Tribes game en route, but without the involvement of the original creators. I think this comic shows the kind of faith we had. In truth, though we had no faith in Vivendi, they made an amazing choice on who would develop it: Irrational Games, the creators of System Shock 2. It was a Tribes game with a complete single player storyline, a first, but the multiplayer—which I actually liked a lot—diverged too much from expectations to really take off again.

HARD HITTING

December 16, 2002 Sites like the one mentioned kept their forces occupied by cooking up crackpot theories for what Nintendo's supposed "Megaton" announcement was. This was a *rumor* of a rumored announcement that seized the news apparatus with a python's grip, and once it had entered the public imagination it needed to be stoked with additional tell-nothing, nonsense content.

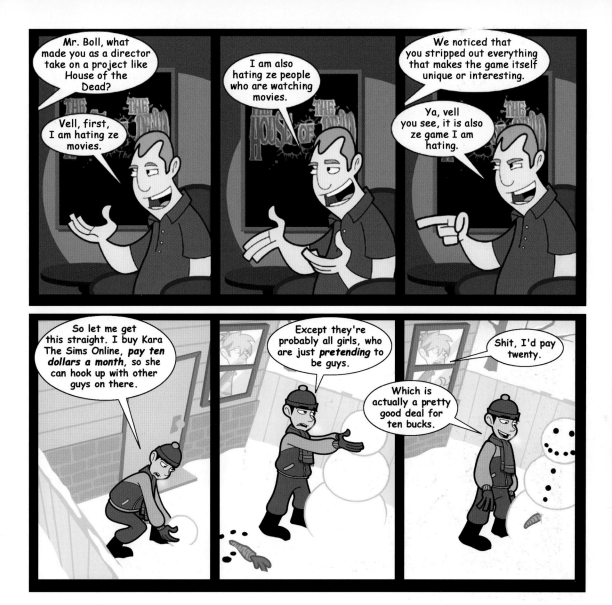

HOUSE OF ZE DEAD

December 18, 2002 Did you know that his name is actually pronounced "Yoo-Vah"? Man, I've got bags of crazy facts like that. Did you know that turtles can drive? That is totally true. Did you know that if you blow up a balloon underwater, the pressure can return through your mouth and POP OUT YOUR GODDAMN EYE???

SNOWMANATOMY

December 20, 2002 As a young man, I had more than a passing familiarity with online romance. In the days before your International Cyber Web, we had our trysts at twelve hundred baud, on local Bulletin Board Systems, and this was sufficient. In the pristine age before emoticons, sentiments were expressed with the entire language. Oh, for those sweet days, when only our people had the wherewithal to "dial into" networks. Sweet Shodan, let those days come again!

WE'RE RIGHT AGAIN, 2002

December 23, 2002 We do the "We're Right" strips a little ahead of time, to be posted while we're back home in Spokanistan for the holidays. It's really nice to have these rankings available now, at this point in the future—I'd forgotten how much I loved Hegemonia. I did, however, recall Gabriel's joyful period as a card-collecting *princess* with perfect clarity.

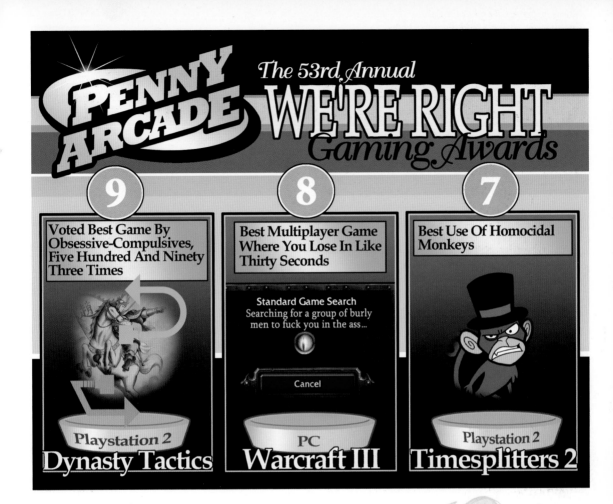

PENNY ARCADE *The 53rd Annual* **WE'RE RIGHT** *Gaming Awards*

9

Voted Best Game By Obsessive-Compulsives, Five Hundred And Ninety Three Times

Playstation 2
Dynasty Tactics

8

Best Multiplayer Game Where You Lose In Like Thirty Seconds

Standard Game Search
Searching for a group of burly men to fuck you in the ass...

Cancel

PC
Warcraft III

7

Best Use Of Homocidal Monkeys

Playstation 2
Timesplitters 2

WE'RE RIGHT AGAIN, PART TWO

December 25, 2002 Dynasty Tactics was probably too complex for its own good, which means that I loved it with every fiber of my being. Warcraft III's multiplayer matching left people in need of counseling. Hateful monkeys were a common opponent in Timesplitters 2 multiplayer matches, and the post for this day suggested that throughout the match they would "yowl in worship to their wild-eyed simian god, who is often depicted with seven tails."

PENNY ARCADE

The 53rd Annual

WE'RE RIGHT
Gaming Awards

6

Best Use Of Racial Stereotypes In A Soccer Game

Gamecube
Soccer Slam

5

Best Game Where Gabe Will Kick Your Fucking Ass, He's Not Even Kidding

Don't Even Load It Up

MECH KING

XBox
MechAssault

4

Best Racoon Game Since Ringtales On The Super Nintendo

RINGTALES
SUPER NINTENDO
ENTERTAINMENT SYSTEM

Playstation 2
Sly Cooper

WE'RE RIGHT AGAIN AND AGAIN

December 27, 2002 We love all these games, which I'm sure comes as no surprise. But there is not now, nor has there ever *been* a game called Ringtales. We needed to imply that Sly Cooper was king among gaming raccoons, and in order to do so we had to invent a rodent gaming legacy that did not (as such) exist.

HERE WE COME TO SAVE THE DAY

December 30, 2002 MAVAV was an Internet hoax; that happens sometimes. There wasn't actually an angry mother's group out there trying to do x, where x equals some crazy old thing. If you were curious how the rest of the awards might have gone, it was Rez at number three, Splinter Cell at number two, and coming in at number one we had Metroid Prime. I still love all those games, so I guess we could have done worse.

BONUS STAGE

Concept artwork for the upcoming *Penny Arcade* video game

On the Rain-Slick Precipice of Darkness

We announced the Penny Arcade game at PAX 2006, and we've been working hard on it ever since. Rather than simply licensing the property to a developer and then standing back while they make the game, we're actually partnering with Hot Head and making the game together. That means Tycho and I are writing the entire thing and I'm doing all the concept artwork.

As the concept artist, it's my job to determine the look of every character, environment, and item in the game. The designs I do get turned over to the extremely talented artists at Hot Head and they build the 3D world based on what I've drawn. Over the next couple of pages, you'll see some of my designs for one of the environments as well as a few of the characters and enemies you'll see in the game.

Our game is set in the fictional city of New Arcadia in something close to 1920s America. The official line is that it's a "comic adventure" starring your favorite characters from the *PA* universe. One of the environments you'll play through is a stretch of slums called "Hobo Alley."

This was one of my first attempts at imagining what Hobo Alley might look like as well as one of its residents. Clothes lines are stretched across the filthy alley and posters are wallpapered across crumbling brick walls.

THE SLUMS
10/9/06

Another bum
and an idea of what Hobo Alley might look like. I used picture books of 1920s New York to help me determine the look and get the props right. Things like the water pump and sewer are pulled right out of old photos.

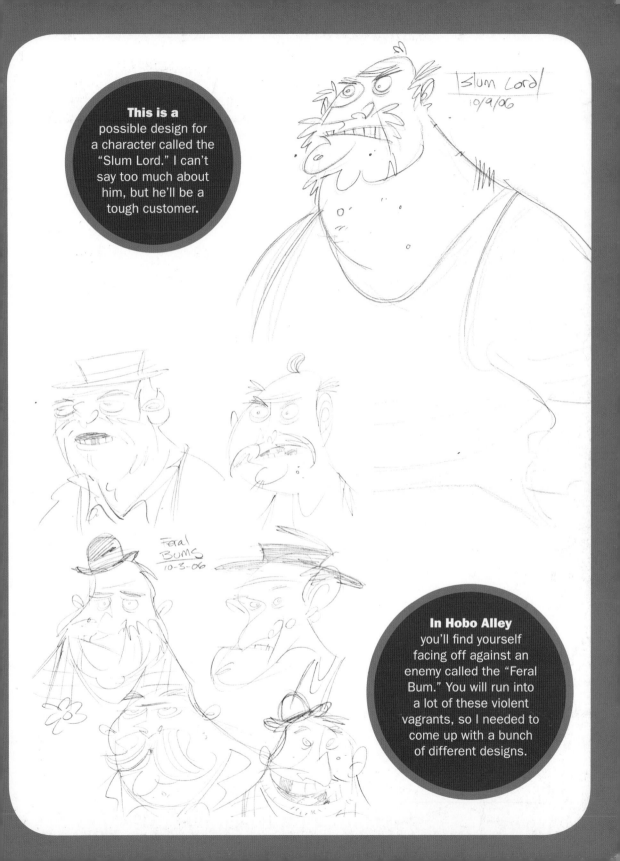

Slum Lord
10/9/06

This is a possible design for a character called the "Slum Lord." I can't say too much about him, but he'll be a tough customer.

Feral
BUMS
10-3-06

In Hobo Alley you'll find yourself facing off against an enemy called the "Feral Bum." You will run into a lot of these violent vagrants, so I needed to come up with a bunch of different designs.

A group of Feral Bums diving at some scattered loose change. As I write this we're still at a very early stage in the development of the game, and lots of ideas need to get sketched out. Not all of them will make it into the game.

Loose Change
10/9/06

These are some very early concept sketches of what Gabe and Tycho might look like in the world of New Arcadia.

-Gabe